The
WRINKLIES'™
GUIDE TO

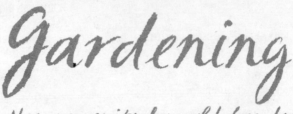

Gardening

New pursuits for old hands

Brian Alexander

PRION

First published in Great Britain in 2012

Prion Books
an imprint of the
Carlton Publishing Group
20 Mortimer Street
London W1T 3JW

Illustrations: Peter Liddiard
Text: Guy Croton

A catalogue record of this book is available from the British
Library.

ISBN: 978 1 85375 837 9

Printed in the UK by CPI Group (UK) Ltd, Croydon, CR0 4YY

10 9 8 7 6 5 4 3 2 1

CONTENTS

FOREWORD

Gardening is a wonderful, and remarkably varied, occupation, so adaptable it suits most anyone's means and abilities. You can embark on a grand scheme or a productive allotment, create a bijou patio or tend no more than a flourishing window box: it need only be as much work, and as much exposure to the elements, as you choose to make it.

If you're new to gardening, it may perhaps all seem too much to take in at first – too many things to learn, too many jobs that won't wait. But remarkably soon you'll find it settles into a reassuring rhythm. The seasons come and go, each with their appropriate tasks and rewards. The frenzy of sowing, planting and weeding in spring; a trickle of flowers and salads through summer; autumn's rich harvest; and then quiet contemplation, with a bit of pruning, in winter.

Don't be put off by the elements. For many a mature gardener, the answer is a greenhouse (though few people buy one quite big enough...). Herein lies contentment: you can garden snug and warm – perhaps seated – whatever the weather, any day of the year. Whether cosy behind glass or braced by a breeze, familiarity soon means plants become old friends as you learn their names and habits, and your heart is buoyed by glimpses of visiting wildlife.

But gardening is not just about communion with the beauties of nature, health-giving exercise and fresh air, or undoubted economies – though none of those is to be scoffed at. It is a chance to drop the pretensions of daily life as you don worn, comfortable clothes and slip outdoors into indulgence. For that's what it is, even dirty, cold and wet. Above all else, gardening is simply fun.

Along with the peace and quiet, it is also surprisingly convivial. Everywhere are others with similar interests only too pleased to guide you in their particular passion or exchange views on this or that plant. Not to mention knowing just how your aching back feels!

Active or sedentary, gardening is a deeply worthwhile thing to do, in there with apple pie and motherhood. It is regarded as "good" by every faith, ideology and nation. And ah, that feeling of satisfaction from a small job well done, the pleasure from positioning a bench with just the right view. Never mind that you'll probably be so captivated by the next task that you don't ever sit on it. For the essential nature of gardening is the process, not the arrival but the travelling. No garden stays a picture, for it's never complete, never perfect. And the joy of gardening is the immortality of being caught up in that process, losing yourself in the job at hand while dreaming of the next.

Bob Flowerdew

INTRODUCTION

*"God Almighty first planted a garden. And indeed,
it is the purest of human pleasures."*

Francis Bacon (philosopher)

*"Gardens are not made by singing "Oh, how
beautiful," and sitting in the shade."*

Rudyard Kipling (author)

"Garden as though you will live forever."

William Kent (landscape architect)

What sage and true advice is to be found in all the above
quotations! And the last may be particularly appropriate
for you dear reader, if you have reached a certain age –
after all you have just picked up a book with the word
"wrinkly" on the cover!

But surely, if you think you still have the puff to do a spot
of gardening, you can't be *that* wrinkly! Then again, that's
one of the great paradoxes of being older and supposedly
wise, isn't it? On the one hand you're wrinkly and proud
of it and, on the other, you're damned if you're going to let
anybody tell you that you can't do something!

Well, whatever your reasons for taking up gardening in the autumn of your years, you couldn't pick a better hobby, or indeed a better place to come to get a good solid grounding in the basics of this wonderful pastime. You may be a senior, but you're going to make things grow; you might be grumpy sometimes, but you're going to become green-fingered; you might query the feasibility of Alan Titchmarsh's perennially dark coiffure, but you're determined to follow his ever-enthusiastic lead. You won't be disappointed!

Why take up gardening?

Gardening is generally considered to be the most popular hobby in the developed world, with millions of people across the globe tending their "patch" with varying degrees of experience and knowledge. Having long been regarded as the exclusive preserve of the retired and more mature among us (yes, that means you!), in recent years gardening has become very "sexy". All of a sudden, a variety of glamorous celebs have popped up like spring flowers after a good sprinkling of liquid manure, extolling the virtues of this timeless pursuit. From the erstwhile pop star Kim Wilde, whose star shone briefly in the musical firmament in the early 1980s, to the World and Olympic champion sprinter Linford Christie, suddenly anybody who is anybody is wielding a trowel and spouting garden knowledge faster than a water feature with a mains-powered motor. Suddenly, your favourite traditional pastime has become the "new black" – so probably for the first time in years, by buying this book you are taking up something that your kids are "into" as well!

The hobby for all seasons

Gardening is much more than just a hobby, though. To the cynic, it is a multi-million pound leisure industry that draws hordes of punters to a multitude of garden centres every weekend all year round, like flies to the rear end of a countryside quadruped. However, to the gentler soul, it can be a wonderful means of artistic expression, a way of improving the environment, and an educational tool for children and adults alike, demonstrating just how important plants are to the human race and the world in general. Some gardeners concentrate solely on the ornamental aspects of plants, while others value their productivity and grow plants for food. Some even develop a passion for a specialized area of gardening – like Linford Christie whom we mentioned earlier, who has a deep-seated penchant for alpines.

This book provides an introduction to the most popular areas of gardening, providing essential information on everything from planting techniques to pruning a rose bush or scarifying a lawn. The book has been written with the keen older gardener in mind, hopefully one who is less inclined to use chemicals these days and who is more likely to want to encourage wildlife to the garden as part and parcel of the joy of gardening.

Whatever your age and condition, gardening will offer you something. It can involve hard, physical work – but if this is not for you, simply turn to the chapter on container gardening. This microcosmic version of the hobby is a lot less demanding but just as rewarding. If you are concerned about spending too much time outdoors in the

cold and the wet, try our tips for buying and setting up a
greenhouse. If, in the past you have been put off the more
technical aspects of gardening because of over-complicated
or pompous instruction, turn to our chapter on pruning
and essential garden maintenance for down-to-earth advice
that will demystify the more arcane tricks and terms in the
garden lexicon.

Plants

The most enjoyable thing about gardening is undoubtedly
choosing and cultivating plants. In addition to the wealth
of practical information that should get your dormant
gardening genes well and truly fired up, a "Top Ten of
Ten" Plant Directory rounds off this handy little tome.
Here, starting on page 149, we provide you with a list
of ten mouthwatering plants in each of the ten principal
categories in which you will find plants for sale at your
local garden centre. These aren't necessarily the boring old
classics – you won't find many tea roses in the selection
– and they aren't all Royal Horticultural Society Award
of Garden Merit (AGM) plants, either. However, the 100
plants together represent a cracking little taster for the
keen horticulturalist, which we guarantee will give you a
warm surge of pleasure. Try a few of these recommended
plants before you begin wrestling with the thousands upon
thousands of confusing choices that you will find in your
standard illustrated encyclopedia of plants; they will make
your early gardening life a lot easier ...

Conclusion

What better way could there be to spend your twilight
years than out in the fresh air, growing and tending plants

and giving something back to the environment? In a few years' time it might be you pushing up the daisies, but for the moment, oh wrinkly, why not make a few of 'em come up the way you choose, along with a whole host of other plants?! This great hobby will keep you fit, hale and hearty. It's something you can do with your spouse or a good friend, or get yourself a plot down at the local allotment and hobnob with a few horticulturally like-minded people. It's time to turn off the television and turn those fingers green. With *The Wrinklies' Guide to Gardening* to hand, we sincerely hope you have a very happy and productive time out in your garden.

Chapter 1

GET READY FOR GARDENING

Right – time to haul yourself out of the armchair and get going! You won't regret this decision and nor will your garden … You are embarking on the most rewarding of all hobbies, in which the benefits are nearly always immediately noticeable and tangible. If they are not, it's normally only a case of waiting a few months before something amazing pops up in front of you – that's the wonder of nature: it presents a year-round kaleidoscope of natural beauty and abundance that warms the cockles of your heart whatever your age and situation. Gardening gives you a unique opportunity to control and manage this cornucopia and the rewards can be limitless.

But where to start? This is a hobby of such scale and diversity that it can be difficult to know the best way to get going. Of course, if you only have a tiny garden or patch to tend, this might not be an issue; however, whatever the size or nature of your garden you need to understand it before you can begin gardening effectively. So, pull on your wellies and a nice warm coat and get out there and have a good look! It's only when you evaluate what you already have that you can decide what needs to go, what should remain and what might be added. Happy gardening!

Assessing Your Garden

The key to successful gardening is a full understanding of your own plot. Gardens can vary widely in size, from a small urban courtyard through a suburban patch to a large country garden. They are also situated in a whole range of different aspects – that is, geographical and topographical locations – which might be anything from a windy, sunny hilltop to a damp, shady valley. Another consideration is soil type, which we consider in detail later on, and yet another is microclimate. Without a clear understanding of the unique factors that affect your garden, it is almost impossible to select the right plants or choose the right time to carry out maintenance, planting and so on. However, once you master these basics you will flourish as a gardener and will enjoy becoming king or queen of your own horticultural domain.

Aspect

The horticultural term "aspect" refers to the geographical and topographical location of your garden and the direction that it faces – north, south, east or west. This has a distinct bearing on the kinds of plants that you will be able to grow. If you are one of those happy, fortunate people who have been lucky enough to retire to the sunshine, there is absolutely no point in trying to recreate the most-likely green and moist British gardens of your youth. Shade-loving bog plants might thrive in Telford, but they won't do terribly well in Torremolinos. By the same token, if you live in a wet and windy corner of north-east Scotland, you will not get far trying to grow sun-loving, exotic plants. Put simply, an open, sunny garden will lend itself to plants that originate from open sunny locations, while a shady, sheltered garden will be suitable for an entirely different range of plants – those from shady, sheltered origins! We are sure you get the picture ...

The easiest way to find out which direction your garden faces is to buy or borrow a compass. If, however, you do not have access to one, then simply observe the passage of the sun during the day – is your garden in sun all day, part of the day, or always in shade? Another method is to use a local street map that shows your house and garden. These maps do not usually have north marked on them, but instead are orientated with north at the top of the page. This should give you the information you need to find out the direction in which your garden faces.

In the northern hemisphere, south- or south-west-facing gardens receive the most sun for the longer part of the day, while north-facing gardens are mostly in shade and, consequently, generally cooler. East-facing gardens receive the sun in the morning, while west-facing gardens are bathed in sunlight in the afternoon (at least at some times of the year – well, if you're lucky ...). In the southern hemisphere the conditions are reversed, with the ideal aspect for maximum sun being north-east facing, where the sun is present for most of the day. This is an important consideration to get your head around if you have retired Down Under ...

There are other pretty straightforward ways of assessing the prevailing growing conditions in your neighbourhood. A visit to a local public garden can provide valuable information about the types of plants that are suitable for your area and looking at what grows well in neighbouring gardens can also help to influence your choices. Be careful about spending too long peering over the fence into your neighbour's patch, though – you know how territorial some people can be! This is also something to bear in mind if you are considering planting a fast-growing, conifer screen as part of your early gardening exploits. The newspapers are full of tales of erstwhile chummy neighbours feuding about the extraordinary burgeoning habit of *Cupressocyparis leylandii* ...

Follow the above advice by all means, but do remember that every garden not only has its own aspect but its own unique microclimate as well, so finding out as much as possible about your own patch really is the starting point for successful gardening.

Microclimates

Along with the prevailing aspect of your garden are more subtle variations in conditions, which are known in horticultural circles as microclimates. For example, your garden may be in quite an open and windy location, but the presence of nearby buildings or hedges means that the garden itself is actually quite sheltered and consequently gets very hot in summer. Microclimates can be ultra-micro – for example, a hot, sunny wall in an otherwise shady garden, or dappled shade at the foot of a deciduous tree in an otherwise open site. These microclimates offer plenty of opportunities to try plants that might not be suitable for the greater area of your garden and microclimates can also be exploited or created to increase the range of plants that you can grow.

As with garden aspect, observation is the key to assessing microclimates. Is there a part of your garden that is always sunny, even when the rest is in shade? This might be suitable for sun-loving plants, or a good place to put a patio. On a windy day, walk around your garden looking for sheltered spots – usually in the lea of a wall or hedge – and also for especially windy areas. This will help you to avoid dreadful planting *faux pas* later on. There is nothing worse than proudly marching your other half outside to view your latest willowy planting, only to find that it has already blown over in the wind!

Creating and altering microclimates

Creating new microclimates within your garden, or altering those that already exist, can open up new opportunities for planting. Open, windy gardens can be made more sheltered through the use of screen plantings. Depending on the size of your garden, these can range from a hedge right through to a deep "shelter belt" of trees and shrubs. Solid features such as walls or buildings can create sheltered areas in their immediate vicinity, but they can also cause wind turbulence – because the wind sometimes accelerates over the solid feature and then swirls and "eddies" behind it, causing plant damage in the process. Trees and hedges, however, are permeable and consequently the wind passes through them, slowing incrementally without causing turbulence. There is also a range of windbreak products available, usually in the form of woven netting which, when fixed to posts, acts in the same way as a hedge or shelter belt, shielding plants to great effect.

A combination of windbreak netting and hedge planting can be especially effective in a really exposed garden, as the netting will create a microclimate for the hedge which, in turn, will establish more quickly and help to shelter the garden. In a really exposed garden, it may be worth considering planting hedges within the interior of the garden as well as at its borders, creating a series of "garden rooms" that are progressively more sheltered. This should probably only be necessary if you live on top of a mountain or on a really exposed coastline.

Similarly, in a shady garden, light levels can be improved by painting walls with light colours in order to reflect sunlight, and by pruning or thinning out the lower branches of trees and shrubs. This will increase the amount of light that reaches the soil.

Styles of garden
One of the lovely things about gardening is that, unless you have the most inhospitable plot in the country, there is such an incredible range of garden styles to choose from. Whereas in the past particular individual styles tended to dominate – think of Capability Brown and the Picturesque or Landscape movements of the 18th century – these days you can go for just about anything you fancy. How about a nice gravelly Mediterranean garden?

(Not too much work in that, if you don't feel like killing yourself ...) Maybe a classic cottage-style garden would float your boat? You could try a Japanese Zen garden, a green moss garden, an Arizona-style desert garden, full of spiky and succulent plants – the choice is yours. The other remarkable thing about gardening today is that it is relatively inexpensive, making it accessible to just about anybody. So, blow the cobwebs off your wallet, get down to the garden centre and let your imagination fly ...

CLEAN SHEET OR OLD CANVAS?

The chances are that you already own an established garden and have bought this book in order to improve it. Naturally then, the approach you take will be influenced by the general condition of the garden. A mature, established garden may have some key features that you want to retain, while allowing for space to be created to develop new ideas. A neglected garden may look like it needs clearing completely and starting all over again, but don't rush into such an approach, as there may be some lovely old plants lurking amid the disarray. Alternatively, if you have just bought a brand new house, perhaps a brand new garden has come with it. This would offer a clean sheet to work on, but in such cases be wary of poor soil and buried rubbish. The average builder does not give much thought to horticultural considerations when he is throwing up new houses. In all cases, it is worth taking your time, carefully deciding what you want from your garden and drawing up a plan. You can also visit other gardens and gardening shows for inspiration, or check out a few garden design websites on the Internet or some books on garden design from your local library.

Understanding Soil

For the vast majority of garden plants, soil is all important, providing anchorage, nutrients and the primary source of moisture. Soils vary widely, as do methods of cultivation and improvement, so a good understanding of the soil in your garden is vital. The composition of most well-cultivated soils is as follows:

- 50–60 per cent mineral matter – which comes about as a result of the erosion and weathering of rock.
- 35–45 per cent air and water – both of which are vital for plant growth and make up the pore space in the soil of your garden.
- 5 per cent organic matter – decomposed or decomposing organic material, such as leaves, manure, garden compost and so on.

The soil in your garden is made up of two main constituents – the topsoil that forms the first 15–30cm (6–12in) and is most associated with plant growth, and the underlying subsoil, which is generally less fertile and not as important when it comes to making planting decisions.

Identifying your soil type

The size and type of mineral particles in soil largely determines the type and texture of the soil. Particles range from the smallest, which is sand, through clay, silt and stones or gravel. The simplest way to test your soil texture is by using a "feel test" (see opposite).

THE SOIL "FEEL" TEST

Take a handful of soil from your garden, wet it with water then try to roll it into a ball in the palm of your hand. Rub a little of the wetted soil between your thumb and forefinger and you will be able to feel the particles that are present.

Depending on what happens the following will apply:

- If the soil rolls into a very hard, firm ball, you have a clay soil. Unfortunately, this means lots of sticky digging!
- If the soil rolls easily into a shiny ball, this means you have a clay-based loam soil. Not too bad …
- If the soil feels "gritty" and will not roll into a ball, this means you have a sandy soil. Good for some plants, not so good for others.
- If the soil feels a little gritty, rolls into a ball but some crumbles apart, it is a sandy loam. You should not have too many problems with a soil like this.
- If the soil rolls readily into a ball and has no grittiness, it is a loam soil. This is a definite result!

Soil Improvement and Digging Tips

In the words of Voltaire's Candide, "*Il faut cultiver notre jardin*" – "it is necessary, [or less literally, "it is time"] to cultivate our garden". Speaking of literally, of course the great French philosopher might not have meant it quite like that, alluding instead to life in general and the need to get on with it. However, in gardening terms, digging – the start of just about any cultivation – is the launch pad for exactly that. If you want to get anything useful done in the garden, it often starts with a good old dig.

Getting Started

So, having got the semantics out of the way, where to start? Well, if you are feeling a bit old and tired as you read this, you could always hire a gardener to do the digging for you. Or a mechanical mini-digger from the local tool centre. But then, if you want to do your body some good as well as your garden – and feel an immense amount of satisfaction into the bargain – why not do the digging yourself?

How to Improve Your Soil

Whatever the particular characteristics of the soil in your garden – and even if you have done nothing to it for years – there are various techniques for cultivating it that will help improve the structure, nutrient levels and drainage, leading to better plant establishment and growth.

Digging over
"Double digging" is not, as you might think, something your spouse does when they are annoyed with you, but is instead a centuries-old soil cultivation technique which is suitable for soils that have a very good depth of topsoil or are light and/or thin. You do it like this:

1 To double dig a border, for example, dig a trench two to three spits wide and two spits deep (a "spit" is the

length of the head of a spade, that is, the bit that does the digging). Go right across the full width of the border. Place the soil to one side of the trench, trying not to get it in your wellies.

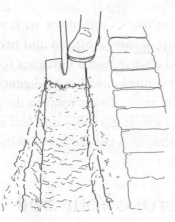

2   Add organic matter (see page 25) into the base of the trench, to a depth of one spit.

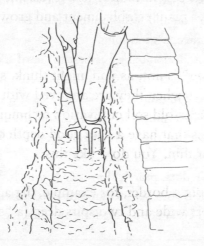

3   Now dig a second trench alongside the first, placing
    the soil from this trench on top of the organic matter in
    the first trench, and repeat the process right along the
    whole border. Try not to get the soil everywhere while
    you are doing this – keep it all neat and tidy. Feeling
    tired yet?

4   Finally, to complete the process, place the soil from
    the very first trench on top of the organic matter in the
    last. Your double dig has been accomplished!

TOP TEN DIGGING TIPS

1   If you have a bad back, get a clean bill of health from
    your doctor before you start digging. No cheating now,
    though – you are supposed to have decided you want
    to do this!

2   Wear a supportive exercise belt or elasticated corset.
    Might as well look like Errol Flynn while you are
    improving the garden …

3   Choose your spade carefully. Buy one that is long
    enough for you and feels comfortable. If it keeps hitting
    you in the face, it's too long.

4   A spade with a pointed tip is best for hard soils – and
    looks "cool". Consult a specialist horticultural tools
    salesperson if in doubt.

5   Only ever use a shovel for clearing soil and rubble
    away – never for the actual digging, for which you
    should always use a spade.

6   Wear heavy-duty, practical footwear, which should be
    waterproof if your soil is damp or particularly water-
    retentive. This is not a time for your dancing shoes.

7　Use your legs and keep your back as straight as possible as you dig. Lower your "spare" hand on the shaft of the spade as far as possible before lifting the soil out of the trench. This way you are less likely to be found doubled-up by a friend or neighbour.

8　Take regular breaks – after all, you don't want to overdo it, do you?

9　Don't dig in very wet, frosty or sunbaked conditions.

10　Be realistic – don't take on more than you can cope with! Remember – you are not as fit as you used to be ...

Adding organic matter

Organic matter is added to soil in order to improve its structure, drainage and nutrient levels. Apply it to the surface and gently fork into the soil, or, when starting a border from scratch, add it at the digging over stage (see pages 22–24). This will ensure a rich, well-balanced soil that will benefit plants from the outset.

Farmyard manure can improve soil structure and boost nutrient levels, but must have been allowed to rot for at least a year before application in the garden, as fresh manure can kill plants. Heavy manures are less suitable on heavy soils, especially clay, where they can bind the soil together even more. The other downside with rich farmyard manure is that it can stink to high heaven, and the problem becomes even worse in summer or in unseasonably warm weather. Your neighbours won't thank you for the flies it attracts, either.

Garden compost improves structure, nutrient levels and often drainage potential. It is produced by composting green waste in the garden (see below). Alternatively, composted bark adds structure to the soil and improves drainage, especially on heavy soils, though it has little nutritional value.

Finally, leaf litter is an excellent soil improver, aiding structure and drainage and adding a degree of nutrition.

Mulching

This is the application of a surface dressing of organic or inorganic matter to control weeds, aid moisture retention and, depending on the type of mulch, to improve soil structure and nutrient levels.

- Apply mulches when the soil is beginning to warm up and has good moisture levels. This is usually the case in mid- to late spring.
- Do not mulch when the soil is frozen, waterlogged or very dry.
- Do not mulch over the crowns (growing points) of perennials or the "neck" of woody plants where the stem meets the ground, as this can cause rotting.

MAKING COMPOST

Composting is the recycling of green waste into a useable soil improver or mulch for the garden – it is totally organic and completely free! Don't leave it hanging around for too long, though – and keep it properly covered up – as otherwise it will attract maggots, rats and foxes.

What to add:
- Grass clippings
- Fallen leaves
- Vegetable peelings
- Annual weeds
- Hedge clippings
- Spent potting compost
- Manure
- Spent annual plants and bedding plants
- Spent stems from perennials
- Thin woody material (less than 10mm(¼in)
- Old turf and topsoil.

What NOT to add:
- Meat products
- Diseased plant material
- Inorganic matter such as plastics or metal
- Perennial weeds.

SETTING UP A COMPOST HEAP

The good old-fashioned compost heap is arguably the best kind, providing it is established and managed properly. Here is how to set one up:

- Choose a site in full sun or light shade.
- Make a compost "bin" 2 x 2m (6 x 6ft) square and around 1.4m (5ft) high from timber or old pallets, open at the front or with a removable section, and with a floor of bare earth.

- Start off with a layer of grass clippings or perennial stems to a depth of 20–40cm (8–16in). Add a second layer, of fallen leaves or spent bedding plants, and so on.
- Once you start to see decomposition and heat generated, monitor the heap to make sure it does not become excessively dry or overly wet. Turn the compost regularly with a garden fork. The compost should be ready to use after about nine months to a year of mulching down.

Using fertilizers

Fertilizers are either inorganic synthesized compounds or naturally occurring organic compounds that improve the nutrient and mineral levels of soils. The three primary nutrients found in plant fertilizers are:

- Nitrogen (N) – for green growth.
- Phosphorus (P) – for flowers.
- Potassium (K) – for root growth.

In addition to these there are a number of other nutrients and essential minerals, which are equally important to plant growth.

Compound fertilizers supply two or more of the main nutrients for plant growth. They have the advantage of being designed for specific tasks, such as improving root structure or boosting green growth.

Straight fertilizers supply only one nutrient in concentrated form. These are designed for a specific requirement, such as boosting flowering in tomatoes, and should not be used as a general feed.

Both compound and straight fertilizers can be applied as either a surface dressing of granules, in liquid feeds or as crushed material such as bonemeal.

Soil Characteristics

As we explained earlier, there are lots of different types of garden soil, which are defined by the particles that make up their constituency. Of course, you could set out to buy a property with ideal soil for gardening, but more likely you will have to make do with what you find in your garden and then set about improving it as best you can. This can take a fair bit of effort, but the rewards will come when you see all your new plants bursting out of the soil within a few seasons!

Loam soils
A deep loam soil is probably the ideal soil for gardening. These soils tend to be fertile, well-drained yet moisture retentive, easy to cultivate and suitable for growing most plants. However, they are not without their problems: over cultivation can lead to "panning", in which a hard layer of soil forms under the surface that can act as a barrier to plant roots, and especially "capping" – in which rainfall causes the surface soil to bind together, preventing water from penetrating the surface.

Loam soils will benefit from:

- Regular (spring and autumn) improvement with organic matter.
- The application of fertilizers.
- Changing the depth of cultivation, to reduce the risk of panning.
- Annual mulching, to alleviate capping.

Clay soils

These are are heavy, sticky and generally a bit of a challenge! Though often fertile, they tend to be hard to cultivate, poorly drained and prone to panning (see page 29) and compaction. In summer, clay soils can bake rock hard, while in winter they can turn into something resembling the Somme *c.* 1917. However, clay soils can actually be massively improved and made to cooperate, providing the appropriate cultivation methods are applied and, above all, the timing is right.

Clay soils will benefit from:

- Annual improvement with lightweight organic matter – leaf mould, composted bark and garden compost are all ideal.
- Annual incorporation of sandy grit, applied to a depth of about 30cm (12in) and then worked in with a fork.
- Annual mulching.
- Varying the depth of cultivation.
- The application of fertilizers.

Sandy soils

Free draining, quick to warm up in spring, sandy soils are easy to cultivate. They are generally ideal for plants that come from hot, dry environments. However, these soils do not hold water well and nutrients often wash away through the topsoil. Soil erosion can be a problem as well, especially on exposed sites.

Sandy soils will benefit from:

- The inclusion of water-retaining granules when planting, which may help establish larger, woody plants.
- The application of fertilizers.
- Regular improvement with organic matter in spring and autumn.
- Annual mulching with an organic mulch.

Silt soils

These are often fertile but can be difficult to cultivate as they tend to behave like sandy soils. They are very prone to capping (see page 29) as the soil particles are so fine, and can also be prone to compaction and erosion. Silt soils hold water well but will often dry out at the surface, which can be problematic when growing plants from seed.

Silt soils will benefit from:

- Surface incorporation of lightweight organic matter, to prevent capping and improve surface moisture.
- Regular (spring and autumn) improvement of borders with organic matter, by single or double digging.

31

- Annual mulching.
- The application of fertilizers.

Chalk soils

Sharing some characteristics with sandy soils, chalk soils are variable depending on whether the chalk is mixed with loam or clay, and how close to the surface the chalk is. The most important aspect of chalk soils relates to their "pH" level (see the box below) as they tend to be alkaline.

Whatever kind of soil you have in your garden, work at improving it – it will pay dividends over time!

THE IMPORTANCE OF SOIL PH

The pH scale is a means of measuring the acidity or alkalinity of soil. A neutral value is expressed as 7 on the pH scale. Values below that denote an acid soil, while numbers above that means that the soil is alkaline. The ideal pH for most plants is slightly acid at 6.5, but there are a range of plants available that are suited to all soil pH levels. Testing your soil pH is easy, using cheap tester kits that are available from all garden centres. Attempting to grow acid-loving plants such as camellias in alkaline soil will almost certainly result in failure, so if you want to grow plants that have very specific requirements, knowing the pH of your soil is vital.

Selecting and Buying Plants

Once you have properly assessed your garden, learnt about your soil, improved conditions as best you can and had a good think about the style of garden you wish to develop, you can give some thought to selecting and buying plants. This is without doubt one of the most pleasurable aspects of gardening, but is is by no means always a straightforward process. To make the best possible plant choices, you should always consider the following before you purchase:

- **Condition** – It should generally be pretty obvious if a plant looks of poor quality. If the foliage is dry, pale green or yellowing, or wilting, steer well clear. Instead, always look for lush green foliage and a uniform pot full of growth. A well-balanced shape indicates a plant that has grown evenly and healthily.
- **Size** – Maybe in the words of those French car adverts "size matters", but a larger plant doesn't always necessarily mean a better plant. For example, in the case of bedding plants, small compact plants will usually establish more quickly and produce better-shaped specimens than those that are tall and leggy, or in flower.
- **Flower buds** – Plants in full flower may look tempting, but it's nearly always best to select flowerless examples or, failing that, those that still have plenty of flowers that are in tight bud. This means that you will still benefit from their display after planting, which is the whole point of buying the plant in the first place! Another consideration is that you will also want the

plant to be putting its energy into root and leaf growth, rather than flower growth, in the early stages of its establishing itself.

- **Check the roots** – Don't be afraid to check the roots of container-grown plants to ensure that the plants are not completely pot bound – meaning that the plant has severely constricted roots due to the pot being too small and is literally suffocating itself to death. Seasonal bedding plants in polystyrene trays or pots may have roots growing out of the base, which isn't usually a problem, unless the plants have become large or floppy.
- **Bare root** – This includes plants like wallflowers. Plants should be a good size and purchased from a frost-free area of the garden centre so that their roots don't become damaged in cold conditions. Choose plants of a uniform size and make sure that they are not too wet. In the case of wallflowers, they shouldn't have yellowing foliage or smell of rotten cabbage, as this indicates poor condition.
- **Mosses and liverworts** on the surface of the compost – These indicate that a plant has been hanging around the garden centre for a while. Old stock like this is generally best avoided, as the plant is also likely to be very pot bound.

Creating a Wildlife Friendly Garden

You might have moved into the autumn of your years, but you can still do your bit for the environment, and for the next generation. One of the great things about gardening is that you can give back to the planet – so long as you eschew chemicals and non-biodegradable materials that is, of course! The easiest and most pleasurable way to do this is to create an environment that attracts and sustains wildlife. You will feel good about helping nature in this way and you and your grandchildren might also enjoy the abundance of creatures that you will doubtless attract if you follow these simple tips:

TEN WAYS TO MAKE YOUR GARDEN MORE WILDLIFE FRIENDLY

- Put up bird feeders and keep them filled with seed and/ or grain throughout the year.
- Carefully locate bird nests and bat boxes around your garden. Don't put them anywhere that the cat can go!
- Do not cut hedges during the bird nesting season, as this can cause the parents to abandon the nest.
- Incorporate a water feature into your garden. This could be a full-scale pond or a small, shallow pool. Water is a must-have feature of a wildlife garden.
- A carefully situated old log pile will provide food and shelter for small invertebrate creatures, which in turn will attract bigger animals looking for food.
- Select plants that are pollen- and nectar-rich, producing berries, fruits or nuts, or which are a natural food source for invertebrate larvae.
- Include some native plants if possible, ensuring that they are not invasive weeds.
- Leave perennials and grasses standing through winter and cut them down in spring, rather than autumn.

This will provide food and shelter for a wide range of animals.

- Leave an area of long grass for amphibians and moth larvae.
- Do not use chemical pest controls. Not only will you risk harming beneficial wildlife, you will also remove the food source from those beneficial animals and cause the equilibrium of your garden to become unbalanced.

Chapter 2

GARDENING GEAR

If, after reading Chapter 1, you are still keen to do your own gardening rather than getting somebody else to do it (!), you will need a basic range of suitable tools. For many men, wrinkly or not, this is the really "fun" part of gardening. Just like little (or even older) boys with their toys, there are any number of gardening gizmos and tantalizing tools that the male gardener cannot wait to get his hands upon. Some are more important and useful than others and some are quite delightfully pointless. Here we give you the bare bones of what you need and what you should avoid.

The Tools You Need

The most important tools in the gardener's armoury are hand tools, many of which have remained unchanged in design for centuries. This might prove the old maxim that a good design cannot be improved upon, but it is interesting to note that many of the tools that are commonly used in gardening today were not originally designed for that purpose. Many of the digging tools in particular were developed primarily for mining and quarrying, with short handles and steeply canted heads, designed for men working on their knees in very cramped conditions. This means that some of the designs that still pertain in hand tools today are not particularly suitable for gardeners of the taller variety, and can cause chronic back pain and other conditions when used for any period of time. If you are fairly tall, in all seriousness this is an important point to remember when you are selecting gardening tools – particularly spades, shovels and garden forks. Having said that, fortunately there are manufacturers that produce long-handled tools, albeit at the specialized end of the market. Although these tools might be more expensive for this very reason, they are well worth investing in if you are taller than average height. One economical way to get round this problem is to buy one of the multipurpose garden tool shafts that many garden centres sell, which come with any number of interchangeable heads and accessories. As is seemingly the case in so many areas of engineering, German manufacturers lead the way in this particular sphere.

Don't be conned

A good general rule of thumb when buying gardening tools is to stick to items that you have actually heard of. People have gardened for centuries and the requirements of the art have changed very little in that time. Of course, the widespread introduction of power tools has made life easier for the gardener and made the whole horticultural experience far less labour-intensive, but the fact is that many of the best traditional hand tools have never been improved, despite the appearance on the market of any number of weird and wonderful inventions. So, stick to what you know and what you think you will need, rather than the wacky new device that has you raising your eyebrows in the garden centre. You might regret such a purchase and you would be better off saving your money for plants.

Buying smart

Before purchasing any tools, it is worth considering how much use they are likely to get and what features you have in your garden that require specific tools to maintain them. For example, a bigger garden usually equals more use, as does heavier soil, in which case you might want to invest in heavier-duty, more expensive tools. Naturally, if you don't have any trees that need cutting down you will not need a chainsaw and if you don't have a hedge, don't waste your money buying trimmers.

Spades, shovels and garden forks

Digging tools probably get more use in the garden than any others and come in an astonishing array of different forms and varieties. You might think that digging is a pretty straightforward activity, but clearly the inventors of the myriad alternative spades, shovels and forks that have seen the light of day over the centuries had different ideas. If you have ever wondered what the difference is between a spade and a shovel, you are about to find out! As you begin your gardening adventure, you will need the following inventory of basic tools:

- **Digging spade** – Designed (surprise, surprise!) for digging, this tool should be robust and have a large, rigid head. Some digging spades have foot plates welded to the top of the blade to make digging more comfortable. Go to your local garden centre and try a few different digging spades out for comfort. You should select one that has a comfortable handle in which your gloved hand fits snugly. Avoid spades with painted shafts – the paint might be concealing weaknesses or flaws in the wood such as a knot or grafted-on piece. It is better to go for one with a plain, unadorned wooden shaft in which you can see any imperfections. You might consider a spade with a metal shaft, but bear in mind that these can be cold to the touch and uncomfortable to use in winter. The other problem is that a metal spade is finished if the shaft breaks, whereas you can always replace a wooden shaft. Metal shafts have the added disadvantage of conducting electricity most efficiently, should you be unfortunate enough to hit a live electrical wire while digging. You might find digging exhilarating, but we are sure you won't want to get that much of a kick out of it!

- **Border spade** – This is a small-headed spade for working around plants. This kind of spade tends to be lighter and easier to use than a digging spade, which is why they are popular with lots of female gardeners. It is vital to buy one of these in addition to a digging spade, because with the latter it is all too easy to wreak havoc on any number of poor, unsuspecting plants in the border.
- **Ditching/trenching spade** – This spade has a narrow head tapering to a V-shape for ditching, digging post holes and so on. Although you might not have any plans to emulate Winston Churchill and embark

on large-scale ditch digging, this spade is useful for digging post holes, as its narrow head means it can reach a greater depth than a conventional spade without making a wide hole.

- **Shovels** – There is a wide range of shovels available, from the classic builder's shovel, through to large-headed, lightweight models for shifting mulch or snow. So, what's the difference between a shovel and a spade? Well, shovels have rounded edges and pans which make it easier to penetrate mounds and piles of loose material and scoop it up more easily. The heads of shovels are generally cast from thinner, more pliable metal than those of spades. If you are digging in hard ground, you will always find a spade easier to use than a shovel. As with spades, when it comes to shovels, a strong shaft and a comfortable handle are the key considerations.

- **Digging fork** – The fork equivalent of the digging spade, exclusively designed for digging. All the advice that applies to digging spades is equally relevant to digging forks. A digging fork is an incredibly versatile tool that many gardeners prefer to a spade. This is because it can be so much easier to penetrate and break up hard ground with a garden fork, as well as using it to dig up bulbs and root crops, including onions and potatoes. Forks are also very useful for scooping jobs – for example, moving compost or hay from one spot to another. The main thing to bear in mind when selecting a garden fork, is that the tines should be evenly spaced and very rigid indeed. If you buy an inexpensive or substandard fork, you will quickly become very frustrated by the way in which the tines bend and separate as you dig, divide plants and so on.

- **Border fork** – This is a small fork with a narrow head that is designed for working in and around plants. The advice above pertaining to border spades is just as relevant to border forks.
- **Muck or dung fork** – This tool has a larger head than a digging fork, with curving, slender tines. It can be used for shifting manure or dung and turning compost.

Hand digging tools

These are, in effect, baby versions of the tools above, designed for close work in small areas or for specialized jobs such as bulb planting. The main hand digging tools are:

- trowel
- hand fork
- specialized bulb planters.

To which can be added a range of more obscure items designed for removing weeds from lawns, for example. A good hand trowel and fork and one bulb planter are usually more than adequate for the hobby gardener.

Weeding tools

Like anything else in life, gardening has its downsides, one of which has to be weeding. To paraphrase Dr Johnson (although of course he was talking about London, not gardening!), a gardener who does not tire of weeding must be tired of life. The sheer tedium involved in extracting troublesome, unwanted, ugly little plants from the soil can be the only explanation for the extraordinary proliferation of contraptions designed for this purpose over the centuries. Sadly, beyond your own hand, a fork or hand fork, about the only one that actually works is the hoe! Again, there are variations on the theme, the draw hoe having a blade at 90-degrees to the handle and used by pulling back across the soil, while the Dutch hoe has a blade that comes straight from the handle and is utilized with a stabbing motion, cutting weeds off at the base. Hoes are killer gardening tools that make weeding bearable and will give you some decent exercise into the bargain. Weeding might be boring, but there is some satisfaction to be had once all those naughty little plants have been chopped or removed. Whatever you do, don't be tempted to get out a chemical weedkiller. It won't do you or your garden any good and might end up making the cat very ill!

Rakes

There are two main types of rake, the first being used primarily for soil cultivation, the second for leaf raking, scarifying grass and so on. It's worth investing in both types, as neither will do the other's job particularly well.

- **Landscape rake** – This tool has a flat head, rather like a hair comb, made from metal or wood. This is the type of rake that has featured in a thousand slapstick jokes in films and on television, that involves some poor soul standing on the end of it and being smacked in the face by the handle. You use this sort of rake for heavy duty soil raking and levelling. You might also use it for spreading gravel on a driveway or path.
- **Spring tine rake** – This type of rake comes in a variety

of forms, but the most popular is the spring tine rake, with flexible tines fanning out from the base of the handle. These tines are usually made from light gauge metal; there are also plastic variants, but these tend to be less well-suited to the rigours of grass scarifying. Rakes of this kind need looking after carefully, as otherwise the tines will easily become bent and damaged. Always stand a rake like this on the base of its handle against the wall, never on its tines.

Shears

There are three main types of shears, two designed primarily for use on grass, the other more versatile and suitable for a variety of tasks.

- **Border shears** – With long handles and blades that lie flat to the soil (rather like long-handled hedge shears), these tools are invaluable for cutting back and tidying plants in the border.
- **Edging shears** – These shears are fitted with upright blades for cutting crisp edges around borders.
- **Hedge shears** – These shears have short handles and are designed primarily for trimming hedges.

The performance of shears depends mainly on the quality of their blades, so it is worth investing in as good a quality blade as you can afford. With long-handled shears check that there is not too much flexing in the handles, as this can be a real nuisance when you are trying to do a bit of tidying up.

CHOOSING TOOL MATERIALS

The type of tools you choose to buy will depend on several factors, including the amount of money you can spend, the type of garden you have and the amount of work required. For happy, carefree gardening, the golden rule is always to spend as much as you can possibly afford. However, also bear in mind the following considerations when weighing up the pros and cons of buying tools made from different materials.

- **Wooden handles** – These may seem old fashioned, but they are durable and have a degree of natural flex. They do need regular maintenance, however, including annual sanding down and the application of linseed oil a couple of times a year.
- **Plastic handles** – These handles require no maintenance and have a degree of flex, but they do have a terrible habit of breaking at key moments and can perish if they are left outdoors for long periods. Expect to get lots of regular cuts and grazes if you invest primarily in plastic handles.
- **Metal handles** – These are durable and require little or no maintenance, but they add significantly to the overall weight of the tool and can be unpleasant to use in very cold weather.
- **Stainless steel** – This is the ideal material for the heads of many gardening tools, being durable and requiring no maintenance. The downside is the cost, which is usually twice as much as that of non-stainless steel.

Power Tools

Often great fun to use, power tools can help to make
gardening easier by speeding up many of the jobs that,
traditionally, would have been carried out using hand
tools. Wielding a chainsaw will make you feel like a
lumberjack and there are many other power tools that will
certainly boost your machismo rating. The most common
power tool used by gardeners is probably the lawn mower,
but hedge trimmers, strimmers and rotary cultivators
are also widely used. The two main sources of power for
power tools are electricity and petrol/diesel, and there are
advantages and disadvantages to both.

Lawn mowers

Lawn mowers can be divided into two basic categories,
based on the method by which they cut – rotary and
cylinder. When you are deciding which kind to buy, the
main consideration is the size of your lawn as well as
the nature of any other grassy terrain in your garden.
You might also want to give some thought to weight and
manoeuvrability, as well.

- **Rotary mowers** – This type of mower has a single,
  centrally mounted blade fitted to a nut beneath the
  cutting deck (thereby forming two cutting edges).
  The rotating action of the blade helps to pull the
  grass upright as the mower passes over it. Rotary
  mowers are either mounted on four wheels or with
  two wheels at the front and a driven roller at the rear.
  Grass clippings are collected in a box (or more often a
  soft bag) attached to the rear of the machine. Rotary

mowers are the most versatile of these machines, because:

- They can cut grass regardless of length or quality.
- They are easier to manufacture, so consequently cheaper to buy.
- Ongoing maintenance is simpler.

Despite these obvious advantages, unfortunately the quality of cut is never as good as that achieved by a cylinder lawn mower.

- **Cylinder mowers** – These have several blades (five to seven being the norm for most mowers of this type) arranged around a central axle, forming a cylinder. In front of this cylinder a metal "comb" helps to flick up the grass into the path of the blades. Because of this the quality of cut tends to be very high, as the length and frequency of blade contact with the grass is extremely good. As cylinder mowers are almost always driven by a rear mounted roller, they produce the classic striped effect on the grass, because the roller lays the grass in the direction of travel. Grass clippings are collected in a "box" mounted in front of the cylinder. The main disadvantages of cylinder mowers are that:
- They are unsuitable for longer grass or grass varieties that produce tough flowering stalks, as the cylinder tends to pass over these without removing them, leaving an unsatisfactory finish.
- They are more complex and costly to build and therefore more expensive to buy.

- Ongoing maintenance costs are higher.
- However, if you are growing a high-quality grass mix and are aiming to achieve a bowling green-style lawn, then the cylinder mower cannot be beaten.

Hover mowers

Instead of wheels of rollers, hover mowers move by gliding on a cushion of air. This makes them highly manoeuvrable and easy to handle, so depending on the size of your garden, this could be the perfect choice. These machines are ideal for smaller gardens and sloping sites, but unsuitable for creating a striped effect to the lawn. Most are powered by electricity, but petrol versions are available which can be used on larger lawns. Hover mowers are also easy to store as they are light enough to be hung up on the wall. One major drawback, however, is that most are not designed to collect grass clippings, which means getting the rake out afterwards. Also, it is normally not possible to alter the height of the cut on a hover mower.

Powered hedge trimmers

Hedge cutting is undoubtedly made much easier by using powered hedge trimmers. These use a reciprocating blade (sometimes two blades) mounted over a fixed bar to achieve the cut. Powered hedge trimmers either have one long, single-sided blade or, more commonly, two shorter, two-sided blades. The advantage of the former is their longer reach, usually at the expense of increased weight, while two-sided blade machines can cut in a "back-and-forth motion" and tend to be more compact and lighter in weight. Most powered hedge trimmers run on electricity, although it is possible to get longer versions with petrol or diesel tanks.

However, you will need to be feeling fit and strong to handle one of these – they are very heavy indeed! It can be great fun to get busy with a pair of hedge trimmers, but they are actually remarkably dangerous, particularly if you're working off a stepladder. You need to keep your wits about you at all times and also to ensure that you do not hit woody stems that are too thick for the trimmers to cope with, as in this event you will get a nasty snag and possibly even a burnt out electric motor. You will know this has happened if you hear a high-pitched whine and see and smell acrid black smoke ...

Strimmers and brush cutters

Also known as brush cutters strimmers are, in effect, the modern successor to the scythe. A revolving head, which spins at high speed and is mounted with either a metal blade or nylon lines, is fitted to a drive shaft connected directly to the engine. Strimmers and brush cutters are useful for cutting rough grass and brush – the sort of longer vegetation that a mower would struggle to cope with. A petrol-powered, heavy-duty brush cutter fitted with a large toothed circular metal blade is capable of wreaking quite spectacular damage. This can be a lot of fun, but wear top-to-toe thick clothing and a visor, as if either the blade or its cascading product makes contact with your good wrinkly self, you might be shuffling off this mortal coil a little earlier than you anticipated ...

Rotary cultivators

Unless you have a particularly large garden, you are unlikely to want to buy a rotary cultivator, but for cultivating large areas of soil they can be very useful and are usually available for hire. Rotary cultivators have rotating tines that turn over the soil, with a backboard and depth control that can be adjusted to vary the depth of cultivation and the quality of the tilth. You will need to be in a good state of physical health to handle one of these beasts.

SAFETY TIPS FOR HEALTH-CONSCIOUS GARDENERS

After all this time you have managed to spend on this planet, the last thing you want to do is to meet your maker in a puff of smoke (no – not the devil!) while wielding a gardening power tool. All power tools have risks associated with their use and unfortunately these probably become greater the older and less agile you become. Apart from injury caused by the operation of the tool – for example, a cut from the blades of a hedge trimmer – there are also injury risks from inflammable fuels, electrical power and so on. Follow these tips for the safe and trouble-free operation of gardening power tools:

- Always read the safety manual that comes with the tool, and never make adaptations to the tool that could compromise safety features or lead to a dangerous malfunction.
- Wear the appropriate safety gear and clothing – eye protection, ear defenders, gloves and close fitting clothes that will not get caught in a machine.
- Make sure your power tools are serviced regularly and stored correctly.
- When using electric power tools, either use a low voltage adaptor or a circuit breaker to avoid electrocution.
- Keep the cables of electric tools away from cutting parts. This can be done by passing the cable through

the handle of a digging fork securely driven into the
ground, a couple of yards (or metres) or so away from
where you are working.

- Always take care when refuelling petrol or diesel
  machines; refuel in the shade and never leave fuel
  cans in direct sunlight where combustible vapours can
  accumulate.
- Always check the area you are about to work in before
  starting. Look out for objects that may damage the
  machine or be flicked up dangerously, particularly by
  strimmers or mowers.

Gardening Accessories

As well as the essential hand tools and the power tools
that you might need, a range of accessories will assist you
with a number of everyday gardening tasks, including:

- **Gardening gloves** – Essential for tough jobs or when
  working with prickly plants. These are usually made
  of fabric or rubber and can be bought at any garden
  centre or shop.
- **Watering equipment** – Including hoses, hose reels,
  watering cans and so on. Despite our fairly moist
  climate (although perhaps slightly more erratic
  nowadays, in the age of global warming), many plants
  need watering regularly in addition to the rain that
  they receive.
- **Sprayers** – For misting indoor plants and applying
  pesticides or organic compounds.

- **Garden twine or wire** – For tying in climbing plants; an environmentally conscious biodegradable twine is ideal.
- **Garden line** – For marking out border edges and accurately positioning plants.
- **Eye and ear protection** – Make sure these items conform to relevant safety standards. You might look silly in them, but you will be thankful the first time a large chunk of woody material flies out of your hedge trimmers or strimmer.
- **Wheelbarrow** – Essential for moving mulch, compost and so on. There are many different types on the market – some lighter and more manoeuvrable than others. Try before you buy.

Chapter 3

PLANTING TECHNIQUES

So, having got the preliminaries out of the way, at last we come to the nub of the entire horticultural experience – making things grow. This is where those "green fingers" come into play, those mythical verdant digits that your Auntie Mabel or some such used to bang on about all those years ago. As a child, you probably associated green fingers more with your Action Man commando figure, the Jolly Green Giant of canned-produce fame or possibly even the American comic superhero, the Incredible Hulk. But now that you are a grown-up with gardening on your mind, "green fingers" are a completely different proposition.

Perhaps your fingers feel more arthritic than green these days? If that's the case, then getting out into the garden and your hands around some live plants will probably do you a power of good. For there is no more rewarding aspect of horticulture than establishing plants and watching them gradually burgeon into life. It doesn't matter whether your preference is for the tiniest rock garden plant or a mighty tree, you will get huge satisfaction from growing either, along with a quite extraordinary abundance of other available plants of every conceivable description. So, pull on your gardening gloves, take up your tools and let's get started on the real green stuff!

Planting Alpines

Alpines – which are also widely known as "rock garden" plants – are excellent plants to use if you are gardening in a small space or in a concrete, paved or gravelled garden – that is, one that does not feature orthodox flowerbeds and borders. This is because alpines can be grown in troughs, on rocks, in pans (shallow containers specifically designed for alpines) or under glass. The tougher, more tolerant alpines can be used as edging plants close to a path, or planted between paving slabs in a patio. Additionally, of course they are very much at home in a rock garden, which might consist of anything from just a few rocks and slabs to a major horticultural feature.

How to grow alpines

If you are keen on the idea of establishing a rock garden, which is a style that is traditionally very popular among older gardeners, do bear in mind that some alpines can actually be quite difficult to grow, requiring a fair degree of horticultural experience and specialist equipment as well as different cultivation requirements. However, in the simplest terms the cultivation of alpines can be outlined as follows:

- Alpine plants that can be grown outdoors all year round in temperate climates, given the right aspect and soil conditions, which can vary from full sun and well-drained soil to shade and moist, peaty soil.
- Alpines that require winter protection in glasshouses, cloches or cold frames, chiefly in order to protect them from excessive moisture.
- Alpines requiring year-round protection under glass, usually in a cool but frost-free glasshouse.

Some alpines require well-drained, gritty soil in full sun while others prefer well-drained but humus-rich soils. Check that you can accommodate the relevant cultural needs of plants prior to buying and installing them.

There are dozens of really pretty rock garden plants, many of which are quite hardy and straightforward enough to grow. We feature ten of the very best in the Plant Directory at the end of this book, in Chapter 9.

Planting Bulbs

If you are new to gardening and are confused by some of the terminology, the word "bulbs" might just be music to your ears. Even the most ignorant novice gardener probably knows that bulbs produce some of the best-known and most popular of all garden plants, such as daffodils, tulips and irises. Bulbous plants are wonderfully flexible and don't just flower in spring. They can be planted in a number of different ways: as part of a mixed border, naturalized in grass (see page 56), in containers, or among deciduous trees.

Bulbs in mixed borders

When planting bulbs in borders, consider the effect
that you hope to achieve and the flowering time of the
specimens you are planting. Early flowering bulbs such as
daffodils, tulips and crocus are best planted in clumps in
a border, where they can provide a real splash of mixed
colour, as they all come out at about the same time.
However, later flowering plants that come into flower
when most other perennial plants are also flowering, such
as Crocosmia and Allium, are better drifted through other
plants where they will provide colourful highlights. The
advantage of planting bulbs in borders is that their dying
foliage, which can be rather unattractive, is obscured by
the foliage of the other plants in the border.

Naturalizing bulbs in grass

Naturalizing – what does this mean? Perhaps at this
point you are visualizing a particularly attractive tulip
being handed a new passport by a uniformed government
official! However, while the concept is similar, the
horticultural version of naturalization actually involves
introducing a plant from another region and causing it to
adapt to the prevailing conditions in its new environment.
Some of the following plants do this particularly well.
For example, the more vigorous crocuses such as *Crocus
tommasinianus* and *C. nudiflorus* are suitable for
naturalizing in grass, as are the species daffodils *Narcissus
cyclamineus* and *N. bulbocodium*, as well as many smaller
narcissus cultivars such as *N. "Hawera"*.

Scarifying – When naturalizing bulbs in grass it is a good
idea to scarify the lawn first with a rake or motorized

auto-rake. This will help to reduce the vigour of the grasses, but most importantly it will remove the thatch – the layer of dead grass at the root zone – which can impede water penetration to the bulbs and make planting more difficult. Thorough scarifying will result in healthier, well-watered plants that will grow taller and more strongly out of the grass.

Broadcast planting – For maximum impact in the lawn or other grassy areas, plant the bulbs in quantity, arranging them in big drifts. This is best achieved by "broadcasting" them – literally taking handfuls and casting them over the grass – and then planting them where they fall, which will achieve a more natural and less contrived look.

New lawn – If you are laying a new lawn from turf, you can plant the bulbs first and then lay the turf over the top. Once the bulbs have died down, usually by mid-summer, the area can then be mown and the resulting material removed for composting.

Growing bulbs in containers

One of the greatest pleasures of gardening is selecting and planting up a variety of containers. These can then be situated around your patio or anywhere else in the garden that you fancy. If you are relatively immobile and find the idea of heavy-duty, border gardening off-putting, then container gardening might well be for you. You can achieve fantastic results with spring and autumn bulbs in containers, which are excellent for extending the season of interest. The best varieties of bulbs to use are those with a compact growth habit, unless the container is exceptionally large and capable of taking taller forms. *Crocus* "Gypsy Girl" and *Narcissus* "Tete a Tete" are excellent examples of ideal container bulbs.

Growing bulbs in a woodland setting

If you are fortunate enough to have a fairly large garden featuring some trees, you can create a wonderful spring tableau by planting a variety of bulbs around their feet. As many bulbs originate from the kind of dappled shade found at woodland edges or in glades, they are well-suited to this kind of environment in a garden setting. Be sure to enrich the soil with leaf mould or garden compost before planting, as shady areas are usually nutrient poor. Plant bulbs such as snowdrops (*Galanthus*) and *Erythronium* in drifts between other shade lovers such as *Heuchera*, *Tiarella* and *Epimedium*.

Planting Perennials

Perennials, as the name suggests, are plants that are more or less ever present in the garden and which frequently offer more than one season of interest. They might do this through the production of flowers, berries or nuts, by dramatic changes in their foliage during the course of the year, or by any number of other means. Perennials, especially small flowering plants, grow and bloom over the spring and summer and then die back every autumn and winter, returning in the spring from their root-stock rather than seeding themselves as an annual plant does. These are known as herbaceous perennials. However, depending on the rigours of local climate, a plant that is a perennial in its native habitat, or in a milder garden, may be treated by a gardener as an annual and planted out every year, from seed, from cuttings or from divisions. Confused yet? Put simply, in many gardens perennials provide the most colour during the summer months, and many are also excellent structural foliage plants.

Perennials always look best when they are planted in large numbers. If you use too few single specimens at once, there is a risk of creating an unstructured, piecemeal effect that can look very unplanned and "busy".

Perennials for colour and height

These come in such a range of different colours, heights and shapes that for many decades they have been the subject of some highly technical planting schemes. One of the great pioneers of colour usage in planting schemes was Gertrude Jekyll, an English gardener who trained as an artist. She positioned plants in blocks or drifts, carefully balancing one colour against the next to achieve a natural, flowing effect. In a Jekyll planting scheme, the outer edges of a bed might start with a predominance of blue, giving way to purple, then lavender, oranges, yellows and reds. In a smaller garden it can be difficult to plant single species in quantity, in which case try matching colours to create a similar effect to massed planting. For example, use five or six different plants that all have blue flowers, such as *Cichorium intybus* (chicory), *Camassia quamash* (camas) *Geranium* "Johnson's Blue", *Agapanthus* "Windlebrooke", *Ceratostigma plumbaginoides* and *Nigella damascena*. Although these plants will not all flower at the same time, you will maintain an even effect throughout the season.

A traditional way to plant borders is to follow a hierarchical scheme, in which low growing plants occupy the front of the bed, medium height plants are positioned in the middle and tall plants bring up the rear, resulting in a pleasing, tiered effect. While it is not a good idea to plant a big, solid plant at the front of a bed, which will obscure the rest of the planting, it is possible to be more creative with plant heights. Experiment with a range of different plants and get used to how they grow in relation to one another. You could try some of those listed in the perennial section in the Plant Directory in Chapter 9, or ask for advice at your local garden centre.

Buying and planting perennials

Perennials come in lots of different sizes, and when you are trying to decide what to buy, it can be quite difficult to know where to start! As a rule, and especially if you are new to gardening, it is probably best to start with smaller plants, as, generally speaking, they will establish more easily and will require less watering. Having said that, if you see a bargain price large perennial that could be taken from its pot and split into several smaller plants, don't hesitate to snap it up! If this sounds too technical, don't worry – it's actually remarkably easy.

Before planting, check the eventual size that the plant will grow to and make sure that you allow sufficient space between it and the next plant along in the border. Carefully slide the plant from its pot, aiming to avoid disturbance to the rootball. Plant it at once so that the roots do not dry out, in a hole slightly wider than the rootball, and the same depth as the compost. Fill in around the plant so that the rootball is in close contact with the soil and there are no air pockets. Firm the plant in well with your fingers.

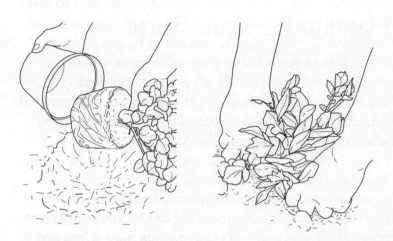

Supports for taller perennials

Many taller perennials require some form of staking or support if they are not to fall over under the weight of their foliage and flowers. The best time to stake perennials is before they have really got into active growth, usually in early to mid-spring. There are a number of different techniques that can be employed; using natural materials such as birch twigs to create a "tepee" that can support the plant, making a "basket" of willow or hazel stems, joined together with twine and then placed upside down over the crown of the plant, or using off-the-shelf plant supports that are made from metal or plastic and are driven into the soil around each plant. Whatever materials are used, the most important consideration is to get the supports in place early enough that plants will grow through them rather than having to tie plants up later on. This is because the latter approach nearly always results in an unnatural, "trussed-up" appearance that will make your garden look amateurish and untidy.

Planting Trees and Shrubs

If you plan to grow lots of trees and shrubs, you will obviously need a great deal of space – far more than for any other kind of plant. Another consideration, given your mature status, is that these plants require more physical work, on the whole, than other species. Of course, there is a multitude of different shrubs and trees to choose from and if you are conservative in your selections there is absolutely no reason why you should not grow anything you want. However, whatever size of tree you choose to plant, make sure that you check the ultimate height and spread of the tree, as trees can often grow surprisingly quickly. Drive a stake into the ground to give an idea of how the tree will look in your chosen location, then take a step back and make sure you are happy with its position.

Measure a square around the base of the pot or rootball that is at least half as big again all round. If planting into grass, remove a thin layer of turf to the shape of the planting hole.

Start digging the hole, placing topsoil in one pile and subsoil in another. When you have reached the right depth – just a little deeper than the depth of the compost in the pot or the rootball or, in the case of bare-root plants, at the nursery mark – dig over the base and sides of the hole with a fork, to aid root penetration.

Mix compost into the topsoil and subsoil removed from the hole, using about half as much compost as the total volume of soil. It is essential that this is really well mixed in. If you have removed turf in order to plant your tree, place this into the bottom of the hole with the turf side (green side) down.

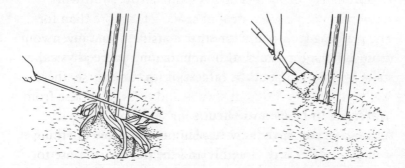

Place the tree into the hole and at this point check the positioning again to ensure that the tree is presented as you want it. Begin backfilling the hole, alternating between subsoil and topsoil and firming with your heel as you go. If you are planting a bare root tree with a horizontal stake, hold the stake in position and fill the hole as normal. Once the hole has been completely backfilled, tie the tree to the stake with a tree tie.

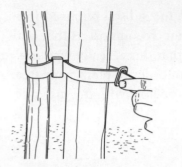

The planting techniques for shrubs are just the same as those for planting trees, although there is no need to use a stake for anything but the largest of specimens.

Watering in trees and shrubs

As soon as you have finished planting your tree or shrub, it is vital to water it thoroughly and then continue watering it regularly until it is properly established. Watering in is essential to settle the soil around the roots as well as providing water that the plant can take up as soon as it is in situ. You will need to continue watering regularly during the first growing season. You can add a wetting agent of expanding crystals to help you cut down on watering if you find that it is all becoming too onerous.

PLANTING TIPS FOR TREES, SHRUBS AND PERENNIALS

Whatever you are planting there are a few definite "dos" and "don'ts" to bear in mind. Follow these basic rules and hopefully all your plantings should establish quickly and successfully:

• Make sure that you create a planting hole that is big

---

enough for the rootball of the plant – ideally half again as big, and the same depth as the rootball. Loosen the soil in the base of the hole and at the sides.

- Don't make the hole too deep. When the plant has been placed in the hole, the "neck" of the plant – the point at which the green part of the plant emerges from the compost – should be above the surrounding soil level.

- Mix gravel or grit into the base of the planting hole – unless you are planting in very fast-draining soil. This will aid drainage and reduce the risk of water-logging the plant.

- Don't remove your topsoil from the planting hole and replace it with compost or imported topsoil, unless you are creating planting pockets in rock or pure gravel. Whatever you are planting will need to acclimatize to your garden soil as quickly as possible.

- Don't plant without first removing any weeds from the top of the compost. Unsightly little weeds can become a major pest, growing out of the centre of the plant. Better to get rid of them before they get out of hand.

- Ensure that the rootball of the new plant is very moist all over. It is often a good idea to stand the plant pots in water overnight – perhaps in a pond if you have one. Remove the plant from its pot to check that the compost is nice and moist.

- Firm the soil around the plant as you backfill around the rootball. Use your hands or, in the case of larger plants, your heel. Good soil to rootball contact is essential if the new plant is not to dry out.

- Water the plant in thoroughly, and continue to give it a good drink as required – usually once a week, but more frequently during hot periods.

Planting Climbing Plants

If you want to add some vertical visual flair to your garden, then pick some nice showy climbing plants. These are some of the "sexiest" garden plants and there are lots to choose from. We've included a small selection of some of the best in the Plant Directory in Chapter 9.

Before planting climbers, first consider the method of climbing support you can provide for them – will it be a fence or wall, an obelisk or pergola, and can you fit wires to the support to help train the plant along? Also, are you hoping simply to obscure an unattractive feature in the garden, or do you want the climber to become a focal point in its own right?

Using climbers in the garden

Growing through shrubs – Grow climbers through and over hedges and evergreen shrubs to add extra colour and interest to your garden.

Climbers in containers – Annual climbers make excellent container plants, so long as you provide a suitable support system, such as birch twigs or hazel wands.

Screens and dividers – Climbing plants can be trained to freestanding trellis or a similar structure, creating discrete areas or dividing up a particular garden space.

Obelisks and plant supports – These decorative items can be used to add structure and height to a border, even in relatively confined spaces. Choose ornate or particularly distinctive plant supports, combine them with dramatic climbing plants and create a really eye-catching splash in your garden.

Sheds, bins and compost heaps – These objects can all be very effectively screened with trellis and/or pergolas covered in climbing plants.

Planting climbers against walls

The soil at the foot of a wall is often dry and nutrient deficient, because the rain has trouble getting to it, due to the building's overhanging roof. To overcome this problem, try the following:

1   Enrich the soil near the base of the wall – about 0.5–1m (1½–3ft) away. Use plenty of well-rotted organic matter.
2   Plant the climber in this prepared soil 0.5–1m (1½–3ft) from the foot of the wall) and water it in well.
3   Use trellis, bamboo canes or hazel/birch wands to create a support structure that will encourage the climber to grow up the wall. Mulch around the base of the climber using well-rotted organic matter.

Training climbers

All climbing plants will perform better and be easier to manage and maintain if you provide a suitable support system before you plant them. Fitting trellis or a network of wires that are pre-sprung and have had all of the slack removed from them will reduce the risk of damage to walls from aerial roots or suckering pads.

As your climbing plants grow, make sure that you regularly tie in their extension growth. Use garden twine, as it is inexpensive, easy to handle and has the added advantage of being biodegradable.

Planting Ferns

Ferns might be something that you associate more with woodland and ponds than you do gardens, but many of them are actually very beautiful and mix well with a wide variety of standard garden plants. You will need some shade and plenty of moist ground for most of them, but they are worth a space in your garden.

Ferns are grown as foliage plants, and are highly effective when planted with other foliage plants that require similar growing conditions.

Ferns can also be used equally effectively on their own. A good one to try planting alone en masse is the ostrich plume fern *Matteuccia struthiopteris* (see page 171). This is a truly spectacular fern that will bring a real statement of individuality to your garden.

Soil preparation for ferns
Although ferns can be grown in a variety of conditions from full sun to deep shade, in general they all prefer well-prepared, humus-rich but well-drained soil. Incorporating plenty of organic matter, especially leaf mould or garden compost, along with grit on heavier soils, will help to create the right soil conditions.

Planting Aquatics

If you are keen to create a haven of peace and tranquility in your garden, consider incorporating a pond or other water feature. You might want to get somebody else to construct this for you – digging a pond can be very hard work – but the effort and/or expense will be worth it. The benefits of a pond or water feature are myriad. You can enjoy the aural pleasures of tinkling water, take heart as a variety of wildlife sets up home in your new feature and enjoy planting up your pond with a variety of magnificent aquatic plants. The only downside is that the grandchildren or dog might fall in, but it is wise put some netting over the top if you are worried about this!

With the exception of floating aquatic plants, which extract the nutrients they need directly from the water, all aquatic plants require some form of growing medium in which to take root. In the case of natural, clay- and soil-lined ponds and lakes this is straightforward, as the plants will simply root into the fabric of the pond itself, in doing so often helping to stabilize it. However, what if your newly installed pond has a plastic or butyl liner, or is made of concrete or fibreglass?

In these cases, there are two options. The first is to line the base and sides of the pond with a layer of soil, 10–20cm (4–8in) deep. Not only will this help with the natural rooting of many aquatic plants, it will also prove beneficial to pond organisms and invertebrates, which help to maintain a healthy balance and keep the water quality at its best. In this instance, bare-rooted plants should be weighted with a large stone or brick, attached with plastic coated wire or twine, and then dropped into the water.

Planting aquatics in baskets

Aquatic plants can also be planted in special baskets, which are perforated at the sides to allow water penetration and root growth. These baskets are especially suited to plants like water lilies, which are deep water aquatics that require a reasonable amount of soil to grow in. Follow these steps when planting in baskets:

1　Line the basket with hessian and fill it with a sterilized loam or clean topsoil.
2　Place a top layer of gritty sand on top of the planting medium.
3　Plant the aquatic into the basket, ensuring it is well firmed in.
4　Dress the top of the basket with 5–10cm (2–4in) of pebbles or shingle to prevent the soil floating away into the pond.

Once the basket has been prepared and the plant is ready for the pond, gently lower the basket into the water. If the pond floor is uneven, consider using bricks or slabs to create a level base for the basket. Amazing though it might sound, floating plants can simply be thrown onto the water surface – that's all you have to do! Perhaps these are the ultimate garden plants for wrinklies ...

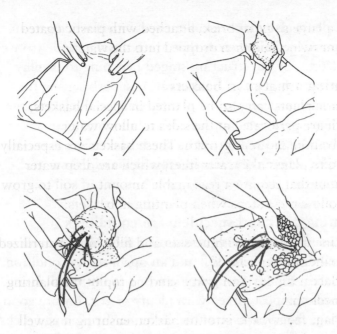

Planting Cacti and Succulents

For a bit of exoticism and spiky excitement in your home or garden, why not try planting some cacti and succulents? These plants can bring an interesting architectural element to plantings and are surprisingly hardy. As the spectre of global warming looms and our climate generally heats up, cacti and succulents are becoming an increasingly viable option in just about any garden. In frost-free, reliably warm areas the larger succulents and cacti can be grown year round out of doors. In areas where winter frosts are prevalent, cacti are best grown in containers that can be moved under cover, but there are a range of succulents that are quite hardy, such as the houseleek (Sempervivum).

Succulents also make excellent specimens when grown in "pans" – shallow pots that are generally made from terracotta. By constructing staged benching to display these pans, it is possible to create a superb setting for these normally very small plants. Cacti, especially larger specimens, are very impressive architectural plants and can be used to great effect as single specimens in modern planters, where they will create a sense of drama and excitement.

Planting cacti and succulents in containers

Cacti and succulents require similar growing conditions of well-drained, gritty soil and an open, sunny condition. In containers, use sterilized loam or a loam-based, low fertilizer compost mixed with plenty of grit. Ensure good drainage from the base of the container by placing crocks (shards of broken pots) over the drainage hole. Gently press the succulents into the compost. After planting, dress the top of the pot with more grit to prevent rot at the neck of the plant. The end result is a pleasing combination of exoticism and practicality.

Planting cacti and succulents outdoors

Outdoors, improve the soil with plenty of sandy grit before planting. If you garden on heavy soil but want to use cacti and succulents, consider creating a raised rock garden where it may be possible to further improve the suitability of the soil by removing it completely between rocks and replacing it with a light, gritty mix.

Growing Indoor Plants

If you are finding it harder and harder to get out into the garden, don't lose heart, because there is nothing to stop you doing your gardening indoors! There is a wonderful array of indoor plants to try, and if you get bored with these you could always have a go at planting up a window box and sticking it outside on a windowsill, and all this without having to leave the comfort of your warm living room.

The only problem with indoor plants is that they are so easy to kill! This is due to a number of factors, including artificial light, central heating and air conditioning – all of which create difficult growing conditions, as they dry out the atmosphere and confuse plants. The other factors to bear in mind, of course, are that it does not rain indoors and your average living room floor is not covered with high-quality topsoil ...

Fortunately, many indoor plants on sale today have been selected for their ability to cope with degrees of neglect – indeed the aspidistra was commonly grown in Victorian times as it was about the only plant capable of putting up with the pollution generated by gas lighting. However, these problems really need not be an issue, as with regular attention and the occasional timely intervention, it is possible to grow houseplants that will really bring your home to life with colour, foliage and form.

Potting on a houseplant

1 Choose a pot that will happily accommodate the size of plant and will allow a little room for new growth. Place fresh compost in the base of the pot. A half-and-half mixture of peat alternative compost and loam compost is ideal for most houseplants, as it will not dry out too quickly.

2 Remove the plant from its plastic pot and position it in the new pot, taking care not to damage the rootball.

3 Add more compost around the base of the plant, gently firming it in with your fingertips.

4 Water the plant in thoroughly with a watering can. Regular watering is essential; with most houseplants, the important thing is never to let the compost dry out.

TIPS FOR GROWING SUCCESSFUL HOUSEPLANTS

Potting on – When you buy a new house plant (usually in a plastic pot), pot it on to the next size up of pot, one that is ideally not made of plastic. If you want to encourage the plant to increase in size, pot it on every other year until the plant has attained the desired size. If you want to maintain the plant at roughly the size you bought it, keep it in the same size pot for longer.

Correct siting – Make sure you position your houseplants in suitable locations. Many houseplants do not like strong, direct sunlight, while others will thrive in the humid conditions found in a bathroom. Be sure to read the plant label and position the plant accordingly.

Re-wetting – If you forget to water a plant, or go away, allowing the compost to dry out, fill a jug or watering can with water and then add a few drops of washing-up liquid. This will help the plant to re-establish its water take-up.

Summer holidays – In order to prepare your houseplants for your absence during a summer holiday, put them outdoors in summer, gradually acclimatizing them by putting them outside during the day and bringing them in at night. Don't put them in direct sunlight to start with.

Chapter 4

GROWING FRUIT AND VEGETABLES

The chances are that sometime in the last few months you have been treated to some home-grown produce, courtesy of your brother- or sister-in-law, perhaps, or some other close relative or friend. Maybe it was Uncle Bob's home-grown tomatoes or Cousin Sally's special shallots? You probably went through the usual motions of praising your visitor's endeavours to the heavens (or maybe you didn't!). Perhaps you looked at the fruits or vegetables in question and were quietly horrified by their gnarled, misshapen and slightly tatty appearance. Then again, perhaps the gardeners of your acquaintance are of a higher standard than those we imagine here … However, no matter how you felt about the way your visitor's home-grown gifts looked, we bet they tasted really good. Because there is something about home-grown fruit and vegetables that beats supermarket produce hands down every time …

As with so many things in modern life, we seem to have come to a pass where it seems the way that fruit and vegetables look is more important than how flavoursome they taste – that their style is more important than their substance. How many tomatoes have you eaten recently that tasted of nothing more than water? How many apples have you consumed that have a vaguely fruity flavour but are really little more than moist cotton wool? This is because many of these fruits and vegetables have been grown too quickly, under conditions designed to guarantee rapid mass production rather than quality and taste. Then, to add insult to injury, the poorly grown produce has probably been shipped hundreds of miles in a deep-freeze container lorry. How can you ever expect to get a decent apple, tomato or grape when these appear to be the priorities that apply to fruit and vegetable production and marketing these days?

Apologies for this opening diatribe, but if you want to overcome these undoubted problems in modern life – without having to resort to the expensive, organic greengrocers in the next town – then you could try growing your own fruit and vegetables.

The Benefits of Home Growing

Growing your own food is possibly the single most rewarding aspect of gardening. The knowledge that the food on your plate is the product of your own efforts, and the method of its growth is entirely controlled by you, holds a great appeal for many gardeners. The attractiveness of "home-grown" food has become greater in recent years not just for the reasons outlined above, but also because of increasing concerns over modern farming methods and the use of pesticides and herbicides, with the development of genetically modified crops further adding to the feeling of uncertainty and worry about where our food comes from and how it is grown

Nowadays, we are used to having a wide variety of fruit and vegetables available all year round but, apart from the country of origin, it is almost impossible to know anything about the way in which they have been produced. Growing your own fruit and vegetables is enjoyable and highly rewarding, and removes the uncertainty that can come from buying them in a supermarket.

GETTING STARTED

If you are keen to grow your own fruit and vegetables, it is worth bearing these few tips in mind:

- **Work out how much you need to grow** – If your children and grandchildren have flown the coop and there are just one or two of you these days, it might be that you don't need to grow that much produce. However, you may be keen to dish out the fruits of your labours, just like Uncle Bob. Either way, give some careful thought to how much you need to grow and whether you intend to supplement your home-grown produce with extras from the supermarket.
- **Start small** – It is better to get a feel for how to grow edible plants and gradually build up from there. Underestimating the time commitment required can turn what should be an enjoyable adventure into a

---

chore. You might have plenty of time on your hands, but you're definitely going to need it if you become serious about growing your own fruit and vegetables.

- **Grow what you want to eat** – It might sound obvious, but sometimes it is easy to be tempted into growing plants that you think you should grow, rather than those that you actually want to grow. Don't fall into this common trap. Ask yourself and others what they fancy eating and grow that. Then you won't go too far wrong.

- **Look elsewhere** – When it comes to the successful growing of your own fruit and vegetables there is no substitute for experience. If there is a gardening club in your local area, go along to one of their meetings. You will find a wealth of knowledge on hand and plenty of practical advice. You might even end up entering one of their competitions!

Growing Fruit

One of the main reasons for growing your own fruit is its superior flavour. As we have seen, a great many of supermarket fruit cultivars are grown for yield rather than taste, and are then refrigerated for transport and storage which can affect the texture. Older fruit cultivars may not produce huge yields, but they will be packed with flavour and texture, especially when the only transportation is from tree or bush to plate!

Almost every garden will have the space to grow some kind of fruit tree or bush, but if you want to grow a reasonable amount of fruit, enough to supplement purchased fruit throughout the season or enable self-sufficiency, a little more space will be required.

Specialist training of fruit trees into espaliers, cordons and fans enables productivity to be increased without the need for lots of space. These trees can also be trained over arches and pergolas to create an attractive and productive garden feature. All fruit trees and bushes will enjoy an open, sunny site with good air circulation, the latter being important to reduce diseases, especially fungal diseases.

Planting fruit trees

Fruit trees are often best planted in autumn while the soil is still warm, when they should be planted as containerized specimens. Prepare the soil thoroughly with well-rotted manure and be sure to apply a balanced, slow-release fertilizer before planting.

Rootstocks – Fruit trees, especially apple varieties, can be grafted onto rootstocks that display distinct characteristics such as compact or dwarf growth that are ideal for growing fruit in a smaller garden, so make sure that you are buying a tree that has been grafted onto the right kind of rootstock for you.

Pollination – Fruit trees rely on insect pollinators to ensure successful pollination and fruit setting, so plant more than one fruit tree or bush and also consider planting spring flowering trees, shrubs and perennials to attract as many pollinating insects to the garden as possible.

Pruning and training fruit trees

Fruit trees can be grown in a variety of different ways according to the type of fruit and the space that you have available in your garden. The majority of fruit trees can be adapted, through careful pruning and training, to occupy minimal space and produce more bountiful crops. The development of dwarfing rootstocks (see page 83) further enhances the opportunity to grow productive fruit in limited space.

The growing methods that you choose to use will be largely guided by the space you have available, the quantity and diversity of fruit varieties you wish to grow, physical features in your garden such as walls and fences that might be suitable for plants to grow against, and the time you wish to spend growing and tending your fruit trees. The following techniques are all trustworthy and long established.

Espalier training

Espalier training is productive and easy-to-manage. This technique is most suitable for apples and pears. Espaliers involve training the lateral growths of the fruit tree horizontally from the main stem, and then creating a spur system through pruning.

Preparing the support – To achieve this, a system of horizontal wires should be fixed to stout posts driven into the ground at 2–2.5m (6¹/₂–8ft) spaces. Alternatively, the wires can be fixed to a wall or fence using vine eyes and tensioners. The wires need to be tensioned to ensure that they do not sag under the weight of the branches and fruit, and should be evenly spaced at around 40cm (16in).

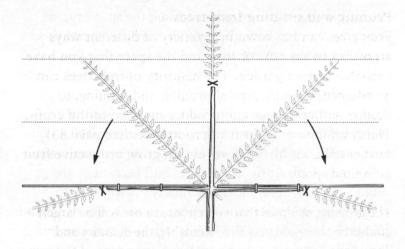

Planting the tree – A young fruit tree with a strong main stem and a few good side shoots should be planted in well-prepared ground immediately in front of one of the posts, ensuring that the best lateral growth is parallel with the wires. After planting, select the best side shoots to train in and prune off any unwanted growth.

Training and pruning – As the side shoots develop, they should be tied with twine to lengths of bamboo cane, which in turn should be tied to the wires, so that the whole is horizontal. The significance of the bamboo cane is that it enables the growth to be tied in frequently and helps to keep the growth straight, without the stems zigzagging back and forth from the wire. Any buds that form in between the main lateral shoots should be rubbed off to ensure that all of the plant's energy is put into forming growth, flower and fruit on the main stems. During winter the lateral shoots can be pruned using the spur pruning technique: cutting back the growth from the lateral shoots to within two to three buds.

Fan training

This is particularly suited to fruit trees that require a warm location in order for their fruit to ripen well, and is best carried out by fixing wires (as per espalier training) to a sunny wall. Apricots, peaches and nectarines are among the fruit trees most commonly grown as fan-trained specimens. As with espalier training, use twine and bamboo canes to train the lateral stems, in this case into a fan shape rather than horizontally. Spur prune in the same way as espaliers.

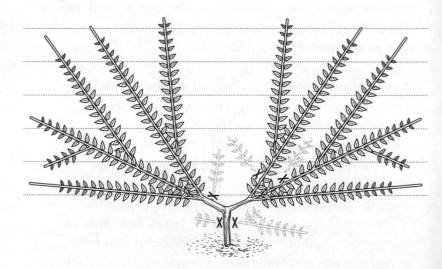

Cordons

These offer the opportunity to grow a wide variety of fruit in a very limited space, as cordons are narrow and upright and can be planted close together. It involves selecting a young tree with few side shoots and planting it at a 60-degree angle to the soil, fixed to a stout post. As the side shoots develop, the strongest should be retained and the rest rubbed or pruned out. These are then spur pruned in winter.

Standard trees

Standards are those fruit trees that are allowed to form a more natural "tree-like" shape with varying degrees of pruning. Apples and pears can be grown in this way, although in both instances spur pruning is usually employed to retain an open, goblet-shaped tree.

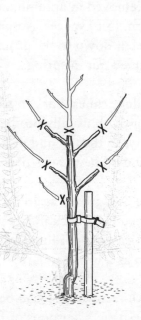

Bushes and low standards apply to the more compact, shrubby fruit that require little pruning apart from formative work after planting. Greengages and quinces are usually grown as bushes or low standards.

Pruning and training soft fruits

As with fruit trees, most soft fruits require a regular pruning regime to ensure a good crop, and this can sometimes involve pruning more than once during a growing season.

Raspberries – Although there are specific summer and autumn fruiting varieties, it is possible to control fruiting by pruning to produce fruit at different times of the year. For summer fruiting, all the old fruiting canes and dead growth should be removed in autumn, and new, young canes tied in at 12cm (5in) spaces. Autumn fruiting varieties should be cut down to the ground in late winter, and new canes thinned out in spring.

Blackberries – Produce canes that can fruit for more than one year, but new growth usually produces fruit in greater quantity and quality, so the old and dead wood should be cut out in winter and all new canes tied in.

Gooseberries – Are best grown as goblet-shaped bushes and then spur pruned hard back in late winter. They can also be trained vertically as cordons, or given formative pruning and grown as a low standard.

Redcurrants and whitecurrants – Can be trained and pruned as bushes, espaliers, cordons or fans.

Blackcurrants – Are pruned back annually to the ground. A third or so of the stems should have all of the shoots removed to ground level.

Dessert grapes – To ensure a good crop, a system of wires set at 50cm (20in) spaces should be installed either in a glasshouse or over a pergola. The vine should be hard pruned after planting with the main shoots reduced to four or five in number.

It can take a lot of practice to grow good, tasty fruit, but it really is worth the effort. Do bear in mind, though, that this aspect of your hobby is very time-consuming and will require considerable expense if you are starting from scratch. Growing fruit is the kind of thing that can keep you happily occupied for many days on end, but if you commit heavily to this discipline, you might find you have little time or money left over for anything else!

Growing Vegetables

You do not need a dedicated vegetable garden to grow edible plants, as it is easy to incorporate vegetables into an ornamental garden, especially those with attractive foliage such as salad crops and Swiss chard or those with flowers, like chives. Containers and window boxes can also be used to grow vegetables, with tomatoes, capsicums (sweet peppers and chilli peppers) and even potatoes being suitable for this kind of cultivation.

Soil and location
The best site for growing vegetables is one that is open and

sunny with good air circulation, but sheltered from strong winds that can reduce plant growth through desiccation and "wind pruning". A site that slopes gently towards the sun will warm more quickly than a level site, making it ideal for bringing on early crops.

As with all plants, it is important to ensure thorough soil cultivation, but with vegetables it is perhaps even more vital, as the quality and fertility of the soil has a direct bearing on the growth rates, size and flavour of the vegetables that you produce. Annual soil improvement by digging in well-rotted manure or garden compost is absolutely essential (see pages 22–26).

Good soil – On sites with a good depth of topsoil, use the double or single digging techniques to improve the soil (see pages 22–24), working in plenty of well-rotted manure or garden compost.

Poor soil – If your soil quality is poor, then it is well worth considering making raised beds, the bottom of which can be filled with manure or compost before topping up with soil.

Planning your vegetable garden

Once you have selected the site for your vegetable plot and worked out the space available, you will have a clearer idea of the amount and variety of vegetables that you can grow. Sit down with a pen and piece of paper and work out the layout of your plot. Carefully bear in mind the following points:

- **Aesthetics** – As well as being productive, vegetable plots can also be beautiful in their own right – and after all, you don't want your vegetable plot ruining the overall look of your garden. The French developed the idea of the potager, an ornamental vegetable garden in which edible crops are displayed in an aesthetically pleasing way, which is particularly suited to smaller spaces.
- **Practicalities** – Vegetable plots need to be both easy to manage and productive. Row cropping is the traditional method of growing straight rows of crops that are easy to sow, thin, weed and harvest.
- **Ease of access** – You will need to include paths in your design wide enough to push a wheelbarrow around so that you are not stepping on crops in order to reach others. Use hard core or paving slabs or dress the soil with a layer of bark.

Crop rotation

No, this doesn't involve standing in the middle of your plot twirling carrots around your head, as much as this idea might appeal, but is rather the practice of rotating crops around your vegetable plot in order to enjoy a number of cultivational benefits.

Crop rotation prevents the build up of pests and diseases associated with particular crops and ensures that nutrients remain balanced in the soil – some crops need particular nutrients more than others and can leave the soil depleted if the crop is not rotated. By clearing and rotating the beds within your vegetable plot annually, you will also be able to control weeds more easily.

Vegetables are usually classified into four groups for the purposes of crop rotation:

- Legumes (peas and beans).
- Brassicas (cabbage, broccoli, Brussels sprouts, cauliflower).
- Onion family (onions, shallots, garlic, spring onions, leeks, also courgettes and lettuce).
- Carrot/tomato family (including potatoes, parsnips and other root vegetables, aubergines and peppers).

These groups should be rotated annually to ensure that the same group is not in the same plot for consecutive years. A typical crop rotation regime could consist of:

Bed 1 – Carrot/tomato family
Bed 2 – Brassicas
Bed 3 – Legumes
Bed 4 – Onion family

… with each group following the other over a four-year period, so that in the second year the onions would move to bed 1, carrot, and tomatoes to bed 2, brassicas to bed 3 and legumes to bed 4.

Intercropping and catch cropping
Intercropping is a way of maximizing your growing space by utilizing the "spare" soil between slow-growing crops to raise plants that can later be transplanted into their final cropping positions. For example, rows of broad beans can be intercropped with cos lettuce, the lettuce being either harvested in situ or transplanted

at an early stage to its own plot. Intercropping is only really successful when the crops involved do not compete too much with each other, so tap-rooted plants such as carrots and parsnips are best intercropped with brassicas for transplanting. Annuals grown for flower cutting can make a good intercrop, and can help to reduce pest attack by insects such as the carrot root fly by creating a barrier around the carrots.

Catch crops are those that grow from seed to maturity quickly, and are therefore suitable for growing in the space where a main crop will later be planted. Catch crops include salad onions, lettuce and rocket.

Sowing vegetables

Before any sowing of seeds takes place, the seedbed should be prepared by raking it over to a fine tilth and removing any large stones. Depending on the crop, seed should be sown in drills (a shallow, narrow trench in the soil), varying from a fraction of an inch deep to a couple of inches. Seed can either be sown at a rate greater than required and then thinned out, which is handy for crops that are prone to pest damage, or sown at the desired crop rate and not thinned.

Sowing vegetable seeds under glass

Crops can also be started off indoors under glass in pots, trays or small planting modules and then hardened off before planting out when the risk of frost has passed. This allows the crop to reach the harvesting stage much earlier than would be normal. "Soft" crops such as salad leaves benefit from this method, as do peppers, chilli and beetroot. Other crops can be grown in cloches (miniature glasshouses that are placed over the crop outdoors to provide frost protection and increase temperatures), or under horticultural fleece to provide an early harvest. Garlic, swede and turnip can all be grown or started off in this way.

COMPANION PLANTING

Companion planting is one way of reducing pest damage and is achieved by using plants that mask or confuse the scent of the crop, causing the pest to be disorientated – or simply not interested. Crops can be also be used to "nurse" other crops, providing shelter as well as masking the scent of the crop.

- French marigolds planted alongside tomatoes will deter whitefly.
- Legumes (peas and beans) can be interplanted with brassicas that will benefit from the nitrogen-fixing nodules on the roots of legumes. Swedes and turnips will also benefit from growing alongside.
- Sunflowers provide good shade for growing cucumbers, or peas and beans will do the same job.
- Garlic grows well with lettuce and beetroot, and helps deter aphid attack.
- Broad/runner beans are good "nurse" crops for sweetcorn and potato seedlings.
- Celery grows well with leeks but will also deter the large white (or cabbage white) butterfly from attacking brassicas.

Growing herbs

If after reading all the above you are daunted by the hard work involved in growing fruit and vegetables, consider growing some herbs instead. The horticultural requirements of most herbs are generally far less demanding and labour-intensive than those of most fruit and vegetables. If you enjoy cooking at home, then having a ready supply of fresh herbs is a real bonus, as the flavour they will bring to food is quite unlike that of dried herbs. Best of all, herbs do not take up huge amounts of space and can be readily grown in containers, window boxes or even hanging baskets, and are easy to incorporate into an ornamental garden setting.

Herbs have a long history of cultivation, having been grown for centuries for their medicinal qualities as much as their culinary value. Today, herbs are mainly grown for culinary and aromatic reasons, but they still retain their status as hugely practical and productive plants, with considerable ornamental value in addition.

Where to grow herbs

Many herbs originate from the Mediterranean and thrive in hot, dry and sunny conditions, with sharply drained soil. If you are planning a herb garden from scratch, choose a location in your garden that enjoys sun for most if not all of the day. If space is at a premium, grow herbs in containers or window boxes, or use herbs such as oregano and thyme as edging for a gravel, brick or stone path, or on a patio.

Culinary and salad herbs

Herbs for eating are best grown as close as possible to the kitchen, so that they are easily accessible. A location in full sun is important, as it will enhance the flavour of the herbs, many of which are packed with oils that become more pronounced when the plants are grown in a position that is in full sun.

CULINARY AND SALAD HERBS

Bay *(Laurus nobilis)*
Caraway *(Carum carvi)*
Chervil *(Anthriscus cerefolium)*
Chicory *(Chicorium intybus)*
Chives *(Allium schoenoprasum)*
Coriander *(Coriandrum sativum)*
Dill *(Anethum graveolens)*
Fennel *(Foeniculum vulgare)*
Garlic *(Allium sativum)*
Hyssop *(Hyssopus officinalis)*
Lovage *(Levisticum officinale)*
Nasturtium *(Tropaeolum majus)*
Parsley *(Petroselinum crispum)*
Red Orach *(Atriplex hortensis rubra)*
Rocket *(Eruca versicaria sativa)*
Rosemary *(Rosmarinus officinalis)*
Spearmint *(Mentha spicata)*
Sweet cicely *(Myrrhis odorata)*
Sweet marjoram *(Origanum majorana)*
Thyme *(Thymus vulgaris)*
Winter savoury *(Satureja montana)*

MEDICINAL HERBS

Comfrey *(Symphytum officinale)*
English Marigold *(Calendula officinalis)*
Feverfew *(Tanacetum parthenium)*
Flag Iris *(Iris versicolor)*
Houseleek *(Sempervivum tectorum)*
Lady's Mantle *(Alchemilla mollis)*
Meadowsweet *(Filipendula ulmaria)*
Peppermint *(Mentha* x *piperita)*

Medicinal herbs

Herbs with medicinal qualities are still widely used
to make natural remedies, infusions and cosmetic
compounds. Many of these can be grown at home, but
it is essential that if you intend to use medicinal herbs
you consult a herbal practitioner or your family doctor,
as some are potentially harmful if incorrectly prepared
or taken in large doses. Many medicinal herbs are also
common garden plants, some of which you may already
have in your own garden. Furthermore, some of the salad
and culinary herbs also have medicinal properties.

Chapter 5

LAWNS AND LAWN CARE

"There's one good thing about snow, it makes your lawn look as nice as your neighbour's."

Clyde Moore (gardener)

If this witty observation applies to your lawn, then this is the chapter for you!

For lawns can either make or break a garden. A really good lawn will set off the plants in a garden beautifully, whereas a patchy, weed-ridden apology for a lawn will look a mess and will be very difficult to look after. There are a number of different ways to achieve a fine lawn, by improving what you have or starting from scratch, and the route you take will depend on how patient you are, your state of physical health and how much money you want to spend. This is important, because believe it or not, a good lawn can take more time to establish and cost more than an entire planted border!

The first thing to consider is what you want to get from your lawn and how you intend to use it. If you have a tribe of young grandchildren who visit you regularly and pets that like making a mess, then a fine sward is probably not a good idea and a hardwearing lawn should be the aim. If you want space for entertaining, then a large area of lawn might be the way to go, but equally a paved area or gravel could be the answer – and will require a lot less maintenance. Whatever you do, make your lawn no bigger than the size you really need. A really big lawn can be a burden, and a lot of hard work. Do you really want to spend all your summer days mowing and scarifying your lawn when you could be sitting on it enjoying a long, cool drink instead?

Establishing a New Lawn

If you do not already have a lawn, or own one that is so poor that you have given up on it, then there are two basic options – laying turf or growing from seed. In both cases the preparation is the same, as follows.

Soil preparation

The key to successfully establishing any new lawn is in the preparation, so spend as much time as possible getting it right. Whether you are laying turf or sowing seed, start by digging over or rotavating the site, removing any plant material, roots, weeds and large stones. Use a rake to break down the soil further and remove medium-sized stones, raking in two or three different directions. At this stage you should also try to even out any crests or hollows by moving the soil around with the rake, or "skimming and filling" with a shovel, taking the soil from the crests to fill in the hollows. Once the soil is level and raked to a fine tilth, you need to tread the site by walking back and forth using very small steps or on larger sites by using a roller, in order to help settle the soil – but not compact it. Finally, rake the soil over again to loosen the surface.

Sowing grass seed

Creating a new lawn using grass seed is quick to do and by far the cheapest method, but it can take up to two months from sowing the seed to the lawn being ready for use. Establishing a lawn from seed is only really possible in spring or autumn.

Step-by-step sowing

1 Prepare the soil by breaking it up and raking it into an even tilth (see illustrations on previous page).
2 Firm the soil by treading it down with small steps up and down the seeding area.
3 Rake the soil lightly once more to break it up, ready to receive the grass seed.
4 Sprinkle grass seed over the seeding bed either by using a drop spreader or by broadcast sowing – throwing the seed across the area by hand.

Having seeded the area, lightly rake the seed into the soil surface and then water well. The seed will need regular watering as it establishes itself and might require protection from hungry birds.

Laying turf

Using turf is the quickest way to establish a new lawn, as you will get almost instant results. However, it is a lot more expensive than sowing seed and the results will not necessarily be any more effective or pleasing in the long run. It really all depends on the quality of the turf that you buy. However, providing the turf is laid correctly and given plenty of aftercare, the lawn will root and settle quickly. Turfing can be done at any time of the year, unlike sowing from seed, as long as you can provide regular watering as the turf establishes. The disadvantages with turfing are the initial cost and subsequent care, as newly laid turf needs lots of water during dry periods for the first season of growth.

Step-by-step turf laying

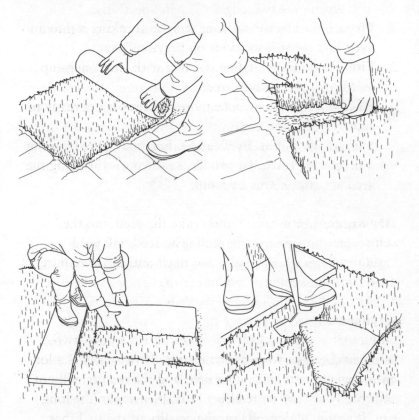

1. When laying turf, start at the far end of the site and work backwards; you will then not be walking over freshly laid turf. Lay turf using what bricklayers call "stretcher bond" – the staggered method used for laying bricks. This ensures that the edges of turf – which are the part most prone to drying out – do not all end up in a row.
2. When butting up two rolls of turf, lay one slightly over the edge of the next, and then cut through both using

a sharp, long bladed knife such as a carving knife. This
will ensure the two edges "key in" perfectly.

3   Use a board to spread your weight over laid turf and to
help bed the turf in.

4   Use a half moon edging iron to cut around border
edges or features such as trees. On completion, water
the lawn thoroughly, ideally for around ten minutes per
square yard, and continue irrigating daily for the first
two weeks and in dry weather thereafter for the rest of
the season. The lawn will have rooted and should be
useable after about a month.

Mowing a lawn

Although many people think that mowing a lawn is easy,
doing it correctly is actually not that straightforward.
First, it is important to remember that grass is a living
thing, not some kind of indestructible carpet that can be
used and abused as you see fit.

Mow frequently – Regular cutting, ideally twice a week, with
the mower set at a height that tips the grass and no more, will
improve your lawn by reducing broadleaved weeds that will
not be able to withstand the regular cutting back.

Do not cut too short – A common mistake made by amateur
gardeners is to cut the grass far too short in summer, exposing
the meristem of the leaf blade to the hot sun and "scalping"
the grass. This leads to the grass going yellow and dying off
and encourages the growth of weeds and moss. So, once you
have reduced the height of the grass in spring (to around
10cm (4in) or so for the "average" lawn) keep it at that
height and do not be tempted to cut the grass shorter.

Clippings – In hot weather, do not collect the clippings but instead let them mulch back into the lawn, which will help to keep moisture in the sward and boost nutrient levels.

Lawn maintenance

The steps required to improve an existing lawn involve basic, good maintenance and regular husbandry. Cutting the lawn frequently helps, but every spring or autumn (or both for a really bad lawn) the following steps should be taken, which will eventually lead to a fully renewed, good-looking and hard-wearing lawn.

Scarifying

Using a spring rake, scarify your lawn by raking vigorously to remove the underlying thatch – the build-up of dead grass – and thereby improve root growth and the take up of nutrients and water

Tining and top-dressing

Next, take a border fork or aerator to compacted or worn areas of turf, digging the tines of the fork in as deeply as possible and then wiggling them back and forth to improve drainage. A little sandy loam, or pure sand, broadcast over these holes and then worked in with a flat rake or stiff broom will help to boost soil structure and improve the root zone.

Feeding

Finally, give the whole lawn a good feed with a preparatory lawn fertilizer. Spring/summer feed is high in nitrogen to encourage growth and greenness, while autumn feed is rich in potassium and phosphorus, the nutrients required to improve root growth and hardiness in lawn grasses.

Patching up

Ruts, bumps and bald patches of turf can also be dealt
with now. Cut around the damaged area with a half moon
and then lift the turf with a turfing iron or spade. The
resultant bump or dip can then be either levelled or filled
before the turf is replaced and firmed in well with your
heel or the back of a shovel.

Wildflower meadows

If you become bored with tending your lawn – and it can be
very hard work to keep your sward in an ideal state – you
could always be adventurous and try giving over part of it to
a mini-wildflower meadow. These are easy to establish. You
can either introduce plugs of wildflowers by digging them
into the designated area with a trowel, or strip back the grass
and broadcast seed over prepared topsoil, thoroughly raking
the seed into the ground as you go. Then, simply let the grass
grow long and wild and, all being well, the wildflowers will
take root in no time and will add a rugged splash of colour to
your garden at various times of year, depending on what you
have planted. Furthermore, areas of bulbs naturalized in grass
or even perennials planted in grass can add a new dimension
to a garden and reduce lawn maintenance. Don't be daunted
by what might sound like a grand design – you really do not
need a big garden to try some of these methods.

Chapter 6

GREENHOUSE GARDENING

Perhaps when you were younger, you were the equivalent of a hardy perennial plant – truly a man or woman for all seasons, who was happy to be outdoors come rain, sleet or shine! However, these days maybe you have arrived at a languid time in your life, and feel more like a tender exotic plant that is happier tucked up in the warm? Perhaps the call of the great outdoors is just not as irresistible as it once was – especially when the nights are drawing in and the weather is getting colder ... If this sounds like you, maybe you should consider getting yourself a greenhouse. You'd be surprised just how much gardening you can do in one, happily sheltered from the wind and rain with a radio at your side, and it is also a great place to hide from the grandchildren, in-laws, the spouse or whoever! Greenhouses are surprisingly inexpensive, incredibly versatile and not necessarily as utilitarian-looking as you might think. Read this chapter and consider giving one a try in your garden.

The Benefits of a Greenhouse

A greenhouse opens up a wide range of opportunities for growing and propagating plants, enabling you to experience aspects of gardening that you might otherwise never encounter. The controlled environment that a greenhouse provides allows you to grow more exotic or specialist plants. Alpines, cacti and succulents will all benefit from protection from wet winter conditions, and will require no extra heating – the glass of the greenhouse alone will do the job. However, if you are adventurous, and you can afford the fuel bills that are associated with keeping a hot house, then you can experiment with growing many different tropical species and create ornamental displays of tender plants. If this doesn't appeal, at the very least a greenhouse will give you the opportunity to over-winter half-hardy perennials, making them ready to plant out in spring after the winter frosts have passed.

Greenhouses are also terrific for growing fruit and vegetables. There are any number of different crops that benefit from warmer conditions, which you simply would not be able to consider growing without the use of a greenhouse. You can also grow vegetables out of season and increase standard cropping seasons by starting off seedlings early. Additionally, greenhouses provide the perfect environment for indulging in the mysterious art of propagation to increase your stock of plants and prepare for spring and summer bedding. This is a subject that is beyond the scope of this little tome, but if it is of interest to you, there are lots of specialist books devoted to the subject. Just try your local library.

THE GREATNESS OF A GREENHOUSE

Greenhouses offer the following advantages to the gardener:

- A place to over-winter tender plants. Containers and baskets can be brought into the greenhouse for winter protection, as can half-hardy perennial plants, trees or shrubs that are bedded out in a border for the summer months and exotics such as palms and cacti.
- A space for specialist plants such as alpines and half-hardy ferns.
- A space for growing vegetables that require protection from the elements, such as tomatoes and cucumbers.
- A place to grow winter-flowering or fruiting plants such as citrus trees that can crop into winter but would not be hardy if left outdoors in cooler climes.
- A place to force plants. Forcing is an old horticultural technique used to encourage plants into growth or flower earlier in the season than would be normal. It's not a technique that is terribly good for most plants, but it does allow you to get what you want into flower when you want it …
- A space to propagate plants. If you haven't got a potting shed, a greenhouse is the best place to propagate and grow on plants, particularly if it is equipped with heating.

Types of Greenhouse

There are many styles and sizes of greenhouse available, and it is really a case of choosing the one that suits your needs best, by considering what you want to grow, how much space you need and how much room in your garden you want to give up to a greenhouse.

Greenhouses are constructed from a variety of materials and the type you choose will depend on aesthetic considerations and how much maintenance you are prepared to do. For example, an alloy greenhouse will require little maintenance but may be less attractive than one made of painted wood, which will require quite considerable maintenance over the years.

All the styles of greenhouse outlined below are widely available. You can normally find several different types of greenhouse on display at your local garden centre or DIY store and there is usually a directory full of other options also readily available. If you want something a little more individual, there is nothing to stop you building a greenhouse yourself to your own specification or finding a specialist company that creates bespoke greenhouses and conservatories. Like everything else in the modern world, there are dozens of these listed on the Internet. Just tap the word "greenhouse" into your search engine and you are bound to find something.

Freestanding greenhouses
Traditionally straight sided with a pitched roof, freestanding greenhouses and either glazed from top to

bottom or with a brick or timber base extending around 1m (3ft) from the ground. They can be made of timber, alloy, steel, cast iron or occasionally UPVC. They all have similar qualities as far as growing is concerned: good light penetration and ventilation being the main requirements for growing plants in greenhouses.

There are a number of variations to the traditional straight-sided greenhouse.

- Dutch light greenhouses are usually made of alloy, fully glazed with a pitched roof and sides that gently flare out to the base. In commercial horticulture, such houses are often mounted on rails so that they can be easily manoeuvred over crops. If you have ever been to a commercial nursery, you will know that it looks terribly impressive when a number of greenhouses on rails are on the move at the same time! Having said that, unless you are considering going into the professional growing business, one of these is probably not for you ...
- Curvilinear houses are made from alloy, fully glazed and are primarily used by commercial growers or very enthusiastic amateurs.
- Geodesic glasshouses are those space-age looking, dome-type greenhouses that are based on Buckminster Fuller's weird and wonderful invention – rather like a mini Eden Project. They are usually made of alloy. Geodesic glasshouses make excellent display houses and are great to look at, but they can be hard to fit with benching or staging, due to their unusual shape.

Lean-to greenhouses
These are good for smaller spaces as they are constructed against an existing wall, usually the wall of your house. In some instances they double up as a conservatory. The one major disadvantage of lean-to houses is that their positioning will be dictated by the available wall space, which might be on the shaded side of the house, thus restricting the plants that can be grown to shade-tolerant plants such as ferns.

Siting Your Greenhouse

Greenhouses have traditionally been pretty unsightly things and consequently they are normally tucked away in the "business" end of the garden, next to compost heaps, raised beds and such like, rather than in the more aesthetic areas. Somewhat counter-intuitively, this often means that they are situated in the worst part of the garden, where the growing conditions are far from ideal. However, in these days of more handsome and adventurous designs, there is no reason why a good-looking greenhouse should not be made an ornamental garden feature in its own right. It could even be used as a focal point at the end of a path or pergola, or perhaps surrounded by a patio with tables, chairs and a barbecue.

The most important things to bear in mind when you are deciding where to put your greenhouse is that it will require shelter from strong winds and good light levels. The latter point is especially important for the healthy growth of plants and for over-wintering, and care should be taken to make sure that what seems like a light, open location in summer is not completely put into shade by trees or buildings during the winter months.

MAINTAINING YOUR GREENHOUSE

As you will doubtless part with quite a lot of cash when you buy and set up your new greenhouse, it is worth taking good care of it by following these few basic tips:

- Replace broken or chipped glass. The odd pane is bound to shatter occasionally – in greenhouses they always do! Especially if you have grandchildren ...
- Check heating and ventilation systems regularly to ensure that they work when you need them to. You don't want that old armchair getting soggy.
- Clear gutters at regular intervals. If the gutters get blocked rain water can run down into the greenhouse, causing all kinds of structural problems and badly affecting growing conditions in the house itself. And your armchair.
- Maintain wood-framed greenhouses, either by painting them with wood preservative treatment or paint. Give the frame a good rub down first.

Equipping Your Greenhouse

There are lots of different things you can do with a greenhouse and consequently the range of equipment available for one is extensive. It is entirely up to you how you fit it out. Your priorities might be just a little bit of staging to do some potting up, accompanied by an armchair, a heater and a radio. It all depends how adventurous you want to be. These days, the interiors of some greenhouses look more like the inside of Doctor Who's Tardis than an environment in which to grow plants, such is the plethora of high-tech kit that can be incorporated into any design. Of course, you might want to do nothing more than to grow tomatoes in grow bags, in which case you will not need staging or benches. However, if your passion is for lots of different plants in pots, then you will certainly want staging, and probably lots of it. Typically, a well-kitted out greenhouse will include the following:

Staging and benching
What you need depends entirely on how you want to use the greenhouse, these can be made from wooden slats or purpose-built alloy benches. You can purchase packs of greenhouse staging and benching from most good garden centres.

Irrigation
Automatic watering can save time and ensure that plants are being regularly watered, even when you are away. Automated systems use a simple timer system operated by a microchip, and are available from many manufacturers.

Heating and insulation
Unheated greenhouses are absolutely fine for many plants, but having some heating – if only enough to keep the house frost free – will dramatically increase the range of plants you can grow and the comfort in which you can work. If you are planning on installing that armchair

we mentioned earlier, you will definitely need heating, because there can't be many things worse than sitting in a damp armchair in December. Ensure that the heater you buy is specifically for greenhouse use. To help retain heat and maintain temperatures, even in an unheated house, insulating plastic – commonly known as bubble wrap – can be fitted to the glazing of the greenhouse.

Ventilation and humidity
Vents usually come fitted as standard to greenhouses, and certainly should be included in the basic specification. The number of vents required will depend on the size of the greenhouse, but most will normally have at least two. These can be roof-mounted, side-mounted or louvre ventilators, operated with handles. However, ideally these vents should be automated, and although it is possible to fit electronically operated vents, a simple hydraulic vent which is triggered by temperature changes normally works perfectly well. Good ventilation is essential in a greenhouse if plants are not to suffer from excessive humidity and the moulds and mildews that this can cause.

Humidifiers help to keep humidity levels constant, in conjunction with venting, to prevent excessive humidity in the greenhouse. They can be purchased from most garden centres. Depending on what you decide to grow, you will soon get the hang of setting the right level of humidity in your greenhouse.

A YEAR IN THE GREENHOUSE

Winter

- Remove all dead and diseased or damaged plants, leaves and debris.
- Replace insulating materials.
- Check over the heating equipment, heating and ventilation in the house. Heating should be set at a level that keeps the house frost-free, typically 4.5°C–5°C (40–41°F).
- Water "resting" plants sparingly, flowering plants regularly.
- Keep humidity levels low to discourage moulds.
- Maintain the minimum temperature in the greenhouse but ventilate during the day.
- Gradually increase watering levels.
- Sow seed of plants that require long germination periods and those that need to be grown on for some time before planting out.
- Plant out tomato plants.
- Sow vegetables for transplanting: brassicas, onions, carrots, parsnips, beetroot.

Spring

- Continue to increase watering and maintain humidity, but ventilate the greenhouse thoroughly on sunny days. Maintain frost-free night time temperatures.
- Sow peppers, half-hardy annuals, bedding plants.
- At this time of year pests can begin to appear – whitefly, aphid and red spider mite – so introduce biological controls, sticky traps and cultural controls to keep problems at bay.

- Sow runner beans and dwarf French beans for transplanting outdoors.
- Transplant seedlings into larger pots to give them more growing room.
- Begin to move established half-hardy plants and bedding into cold frames to allow them to harden off.
- Feed plants with a balanced liquid feed.
- Tie in the shoots of tomatoes.
- Plant out tender perennials.

Summer
- Ventilate constantly during the day and on warm evenings.
- Turn off heaters.
- Plant out bedding plants
- Water twice or three times daily as needed, and damp down the floor.
- Feed tomatoes.
- Begin to take semi-ripe cuttings.
- Put over wintering plants outdoors.
- Remove insulating materials
- Harvest cucumbers and tomatoes as they ripen.
- Pinch out tomatoes to encourage bushy growth, and cucumber laterals.
- Add additional shading inside the house if needed, using mesh netting.
- Sow spring flowering annuals.
- Begin to plant in pots winter and spring-flowering bulbs such as tulips, hyacinths and daffodils (*Narcissus*).
- Mulch tomatoes, apply a high potash liquid feed to flowering plants.

Autumn

- Begin to reduce watering and stop damping down, continue to ventilate on warm days.
- Check over heaters to make sure they work, and be aware of night-time temperature drops.
- Reduce shading by removing mesh netting.
- Take cuttings from bedding plants and tender perennials
- Bring half-hardy plants that have been outdoors for the summer back indoors.
- Remove tomato plants and growing bags to the compost heap
- Pot on spring-flowering plants.
- Begin to take hardwood cuttings.
- Remove the shading from the outside of the greenhouse.
- Feed spring-flowering plants.
- Clear up any dead or decaying plant matter.
- Sow lettuce for early cropping.

Chapter 7

CONTAINER GARDENING

"O Cruelty! To steal my basil-pot away from me!"
John Keats (poet)

If occasionally the sheer scale of your garden gets beyond you and the never-ending task that is gardening begins to feel a little like painting the Forth Bridge, why not turn your hand to the microcosmic and considerably less demanding version of this hobby that is container gardening? There will be days when your you feel tired and the prospect of another day's digging, mowing, pruning or tending to the greenhouse might all seem a little much. However, you can assuage your conscience, slake your creative juices and wiggle your green fingers simply by planting up a few pots and pans instead!

Planting in containers offers tremendous scope for growing different plants, either individually or in groups, as the conditions in a container are easier to control and manipulate than those for an entire garden. For example, containers can be moved indoors or wrapped up in winter, and the growing medium can be altered more readily. Containers can be used as a means of growing plants that you might love to have in your garden but that your soil or the prevailing climate preclude – such as Rhododendron, Pieris and Camellia, all of which require ericaceous compost – but also as a means of maintaining seasonality through the use of bedding plants.

Containers also offer the potential to experiment with different plants and to decorate awkward parts of the garden where you cannot get plants to "take" in the soil on the ground. There is also no limit to the range of containers that you can use – anything from an old kettle to a car tyre can be planted up and made to look interesting, and a trip to any garden centre will reveal literally hundreds of choices, from traditional terracotta pots and amphorae to stylish, geometrically shaped aluminium cubes and boxes. Containers can be used to decorate terraces and patios or just about any other part of the garden. They can be mounted on plinths or set on the top of walls, and window boxes and hanging baskets offer interesting alternatives. It can be as much fun selecting or identifying a possible container as it is planting it up and making it look good! The choice is yours, and whereas if the weather is foul normal gardening is not an option, you can happily plant up pots and containers in your shed, greenhouse or in the comfort of your kitchen.

Types of container

So, where to start? One of the problems associated with such great diversity is knowing what to select! For you can now choose from a huge range of pots and planters designed for every style of garden. However, some containers are more suited to certain situations and plantings than others. For example, in colder gardens, permanent displays should be made in large pots with good thermal insulation to protect the roots of the plants from frost. A good choice here is heavy wooden barrels. Similarly, non-porous pots, including those made from glazed terracotta, are useful in hot, dry spots, because the plants in them will need less frequent watering. Finally, if you only have a balcony, veranda or roof garden with a limited load-bearing capacity, you might want to consider using lightweight, plastic containers.

Terracotta pots

These are possibly the most conventional and popular of all garden containers. They look good just about anywhere, but have the disadvantage of being porous and therefore drying out quickly. You can counter this by lining them with plastic sheeting, while keeping the drainage holes uncovered. Look for stoneware and terracotta pots with a frost-proof guarantee, so that they won't crack at the first sign of winter weather.

Glazed ceramic pots

These look good in bright colours and patterns, and are generally frost proof because the glaze prevents moisture from permeating the clay that they are made from. Check for crazing or blistering of the glaze and be wary of purchasing pots from countries with hot climates that might not perform as well in exposed conditions.

Wooden barrels

Large hardwood barrels made from oak look particularly good in country and cottage gardens. They are great for big plants because they are generally pretty capacious and allow lots of room for root development. They do require some maintenance during the winter – normally just a coat of wood preservative or paint – and can be waterproofed with bitumastic paint to enable you to create miniature water gardens.

Metal planters

In recent years galvanized aluminium boxes have become very fashionable, adorning the patios and verandas of a thousand trendy gastro pubs, among other places. The only problem with these planters is that they conduct heat extremely efficiently and are likely to cook the rootballs of plants in hot weather. This problem can be countered to a certain extent by lining these containers with layers of bubble plastic insulation or polystyrene sheeting prior to planting. However, make sure you water any plants in metal containers very thoroughly during the summer months.

Plastic containers

Some fantastic copies of classical lead and metalwork urns, as well as terracotta amphorae and even stone pots, can now be bought in life-like-looking plastic. These are obviously a lot cheaper than the real thing

and considerably more lightweight! Be careful, though –
quality is incredibly variable and a poor plastic pot will
look really tacky, letting down your entire garden.

Stone pots and containers

Stone is expensive and heavy, but if you have the budget
and the space in your garden, fewer things will look more
magnificent than some really stylish large stone pots and
containers. If that's not the case, again copies made from
concrete or reconstituted stone can look good and will
leave you more money to spend on plants. You can always
artificially weather new looking pots like this by painting
them with live yoghurt or liquid manure, which will
attract green algae very quickly.

Alternative pots

If you are someone who likes to break the mould
occasionally or maybe even be a touch controversial,
why not go for something a little out of the ordinary?
After all, just about every garden features terracotta
pots or wooden barrels, why should yours? There is
really no limit to what you can use as a container for
many plants, so why not recycle an old wheelbarrow,
a Wellington boot, a drainpipe – or maybe even an old
toilet, commode or chamberpot – that should get the
neighbours talking!

HOW TO PLANT A CONTAINER

Planting your containers correctly in the first place will save you hours of watering come summertime.

Drainage – Ensure good drainage by placing crocks in the base of the container. Traditionally these were broken clay pots, but if the container is large and you are seeking to reduce its overall weight, you could use polystyrene packaging as an alternative.

Fill up with compost – When the container is three-quarters full of compost, set out the plants and then top up around them, ensuring that the finished compost level is at least 5cm (2in) below the rim of the container. This will create a reservoir when watering, whereas filling the container with compost to the brim will cause water to run off.

Wetting agent – Mix a loam-based compost with a wetting agent. These are granules that expand into jelly when watered, and then release the water to the plants gradually over time. They can save an awful lot of time with the watering can!

Winter positioning – During winter, place containers with less hardy subjects against the wall of your house, in the "rain shadow" beneath the overhanging eaves of the roof. This will protect the plants against frost damage.

What to Plant

Conventional container and window box plantings are usually based on fairly standard annual plants such as Impatiens, bedding Lobelia, Verbena, Petunia and Argyranthemum – but why not try something a little more daring?

Making a statement

Bold architectural plants are excellent subjects for containers, and for centuries box (*Buxus sempervirens*) and bay (*Laurus nobilis*) have been hugely popular choices. However, there are other, equally structural plants that are well worth trying as an alternative. *Viburnum tinus* cultivars make superb container plants, producing an abundance of flowers during late winter and early spring, and responding well to formative pruning, which should be carried out during mid-summer. Shady corners can be illuminated with variegated evergreens such as *Elaeagnus* x *ebbingei* "Maculata" and "Gilt Edge".

Using grasses for form

Ornamental grasses work superbly in containers, particularly the late flowering *Panicum virgatum* "Rubrum", with its bluish green leaves stained with red. *Calamagrostis* "Karl Foerster" creates a superb vertical accent, its purplish inflorescences gradually turning to the colour of straw, and remaining attractive all through winter.

Ornamental grasses generally have really dramatic foliage, so they can be used to combine and contrast with the colour and form of other plants as well as the style of the container in which they are planted. For example, the powder blue *Elymus magellenicus* is stunning when planted against galvanized zinc or gunmetal grey, while the golden-variegated, shade tolerant *Hakonechloa macra* "Aureola" complements everything from terracotta to wooden half-barrels. There are many other equally exotic grasses to choose from.

Exotic plants

If you followed the advice in the previous chapter and have established a greenhouse, there is no end to what you can do with containers and any number of different plants throughout the year. The great beauty of containers is that they can easily be moved from a patio or any other part of the garden into a greenhouse at the first sign of bad weather. This means that even the most tender and exotic plants from foreign climates can be exhibited in containers outside during the summer months and then safely overwintered in a greenhouse as necessary.

However, if you don't have a greenhouse, there are several hardy plants that can be used in containers to create the same ambience, without recourse to winter cover. *Chamaerops humilis*, the fishtail palm, is compact in growth at around 1.8m (6ft) or so, and has broad pinnate leaves of greyish green. These can add an air of the exotic to the most mundane setting and this plant offers the added advantage of being hardy down to minus double figures. Several dwarf forms of *Phormium tenax* can also be used for this purpose. These plants look great in containers of all kinds. Contrarily, for a dry sunny spot, *Agave americana* is a good container specimen, although it is very spiky, so your pets and grandchildren will need to watch out!

Succulents

For the ultimate in low-maintenance containers, plant shallow clay "pans" with succulents such as houseleeks (Sempervivum) and Lewisia, which require little irrigation and no feeding. To create a strong visual impact, these fairly small plants are best displayed in quantity. Succulents are also a good choice for growing in window boxes.

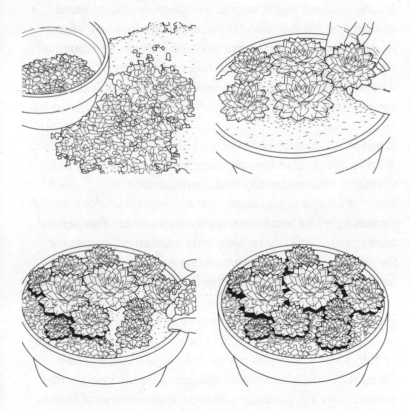

Spring bulbs

Dwarf daffodils (Narcissus), crocuses, snowdrops (Galanthus) and *Sternbergia lutea* are all suitable for containers and window boxes, brightening patios and walls with their vibrant spring colours. You can combine these with evergreen foliage plants for contrast.

Autumn bulbs

Exotic autumn bulbs such as *Nerine bowdenii, Tulbaghia violacea* and *Amaryllis* "Johannesburg" can be difficult to grow in gardens that are cool and damp, but they will do well when they are planted in a container or window box with plenty of gritty compost and set out in a dry, hot, sunny spot.

Container plants for winter interest

A container planted with a stem colour shrub such as Cornus "Midwinter Fire" or *Rubus thibetanus* "Silver Fern" with the ornamental grass *Pennisetum alopecuroides* "Hameln", or *Chasmanthium latifolium* and trailing variegated ivy will provide plenty of interest during the winter months. Other good plants for winter containers are *Cyclamen persicum* and *Solanum pseudocapsicum*.

Hanging Baskets and Wall Mangers

Hanging baskets and wall mangers offer another opportunity for planting and are especially useful for covering up an unattractive wall or building. They come in a variety of sizes and styles, and which you choose will very much depend upon whether you need it to be easily lifted down for watering, and how strong the support is – a bracket or two attached to a brick wall will be able to take far more weight than, say, a hook screwed into the wooden eaves.

Traditional hanging-basket and wall-manger plants are much the same as those used in traditional containers, primarily annual bedding plants, and certainly a basket filled with trailing petunias is a lovely sight. However, as with containers and window boxes, you might want to consider trying less obvious plants. Succulents in particular can make a very unusual and dynamic hanging basket or wall manger display.

GREAT PLANTS FOR HANGING BASKETS AND WALL MANGERS

Lobelia "Fountain Mixture Trailing" – red, pink, white and mauve flowers.

Dichondra "Silver Falls" – trailing foliage plant with silver leaves.

Sweet pea "Pink Cupid" – fragrant pink flowers on compact plants.

Petunia "Purple Velvet" – rich purple flowers appear on long stems.

Begonia "Chanson Pink" – long stems with blousy pink blooms.

If planting a winter basket, try winter pansies, primula, trailing ivy, heathers and dwarf conifers. Underplant with dwarf bulbs such as narcissus, tulips and iris for a spring display.

Planting up a hanging basket

First of all, place the empty hanging basket on a large
(5 or 10 litre /10 or 20 pint/) pot, on a table top. The
pot will enable you to turn the basket around without
damaging any plants in the base of the basket. If you do
not have a suitable pot, rest the basket on the table.

1   Line the basket with a decorative material such as fake
    sphagnum moss, coir fibre or a purpose-made decorative
    liner. Cut a round piece of plastic from an old compost
    bag that will sit inside the decorative lining.
2   Put a few handfuls of compost, mixed with wetting
    agent, into the base of the basket.
3   Begin to plant the base of the basket with trailing
    plants. Push the plants through the plastic lining
    – having first cut out a hole – and the outer decorative
    lining, and to help do this and protect the plants, wrap
    the foliage of the plant in a square of plastic cut from a
    compost bag.
4   Once you have planted one "ring" of plants, add a
    few more handfuls of compost and repeat the process,
    staggering the rows of plants for a more even and
    natural look. By the time the basket is two thirds full
    of compost it will be time to put in the plants that will
    fill the top of the basket. Water the basket thoroughly
    after hanging, to keep the weight down and make it
    easier to lift.

Chapter 8

PRUNING AND MAINTENANCE TECHNIQUES

It is probably safe to assume that you are reasonably interested in gardening, purely by the fact that you are reading this book. Consequently, at some time or another you have almost certainly watched the magnificent *Gardener's World* programme on BBC television. Even if you can't recall founding presenter Percy Thrower in his suit and tie, then you're bound to remember the incomparable Geoff Hamilton, and who could possibly ever have avoided the ubiquitous Alan Titchmarsh?! If you have watched the programme more than once, you are likely to have witnessed a highly technical-sounding and incredibly arcane feature on pruning some tree or shrub or another. Perhaps, like this author, you have marvelled at the precision of the cuts, the angles at which they should be made and their precise positions in relation to stems, buds and flowers. Maybe you began to feel as if you were watching some superhuman member of a race

of gardening overlords, who would understand the many
dark facets and unfathomable mysteries of pruning in a
way that you would never be able to master! Well, perhaps
that is overstating things slightly, but it is certainly a little
intimidating!

Can pruning in the garden really be so difficult, so
complex? Well, as your experience probably tells you
about so many other things, the answer is a resounding
"no". Yes, pruning is an essential gardening technique
that prolongs the life of plants, keeps them in the best
of health and ensures that they remain as productive
as possible, but it really is not as difficult and as
complicated as it is sometimes made to appear. Read this
chapter carefully and we will demystify this most crucial
of the gardener's arts, so that next time you wield your
secateurs, shears or pruning saw, you will do so with a
newfound sense of confidence and cheer in your heart!
We'll cover a few less daunting aspects of basic garden
maintenance, too.

Getting Started

There are few, if any, ornamental plants that will perform
to their best without some form of intervention by the
gardener, and in this chapter we will look at how to get
the best from your garden by ensuring you are maintaining
them correctly.

Taking care of the plants in your garden will make sure
that they thrive for as long as possible, flower and fruit
well, help to reduce the risks of pests and diseases and

keep your garden looking in prime condition. This is the very essence of gardening.

PRUNING TOOLS

A vast number of tools are at the gardener' disposal for pruning plants, but you are unlikely to need all of them. Here are a few of those that are most commonly used.

- Secateurs are used to prune soft shoots and small woody stems, with either a scissors-like bypass cutting action or an anvil cut. They are probably the most important garden tool, so it is worth investing in a pair of the best quality you can afford. You might need more than one pair, as you will do a lot of pruning with secateurs.
- Loppers are used for pruning material that is too big to be cut with secateurs. Like secateurs, they are available with either a bypass or an anvil cutting action. Some loppers have extendable arms, which are handy for pruning tall branches. You can have great fun with loppers, but your arms will know they have done some work at the end of the day and the following morning!
- Pruning saws come in a variety of sizes and styles. The Grecian saw is a small, one-handed saw with a sharply toothed, slightly curving blade. It makes short work of limbs too big for loppers, and is ideal for using in small, tight spaces. Bow saws are used for larger branches and for felling small trees, and range from compact to very large two-person saws. Saw teeth need sharpening regularly in order to remain effective.

- You will also need a step ladder and possibly a full-size ladder, depending on the size and nature of your garden. We are not going to lecture you here about the dangers of using such things, but let's just say that ladders become more hazardous the older and more unsteady you are on your feet ... If in any doubt at all, it is safest to "get a man in" to prune any particularly high, awkward branches or stems.

Pruning Trees and Shrubs

There are several good reasons for carrying out regular pruning on trees and shrubs – to increase flowering and fruiting, to control disease and to control the size and shape of the plant in question.

Pruning to maintain vigour

Shrubs such as Forsythia and Viburnum need to have older wood pruned out annually in order to maintain vigour and the production of flowering wood. These are shrubs that develop new shoots from the base of the plant, which tend to produce more flower and fruit than the older wood. Left unpruned, these plants will soon become congested, the older wood reducing the opportunity for new shoots to form. Every year after flowering cut out around one third of the old wood at the base of the plant.

Pruning for Flower and Fruit

A great many plants including ornamental fruit trees such as *Malus* (apple) will produce more flower and fruit when correctly pruned.

As a general rule, plants that flower early in the season produce their flowering wood and buds during the previous growing year, while those that flower late in the season flower on that same season's wood. Therefore, early-flowering plants should be pruned as soon as they have finished flowering, while late-season flowering plants can be pruned at the start of the growing season. This is not always the case, but it does apply in the main. Check the label that comes with any plant you are buying so that you know what its pruning requirements are in advance.

Pruning for foliage effect

There are a number of shrubs, for example the smoke bush (*Cotinus coggygria*), that can be manipulated through pruning, exchanging flowers and smaller leaves for no flowers but much enlarged leaves. This type of pruning is usually carried out in late winter or early spring and involves cutting the plant back quite hard, either to a framework of main branches, removing any twiggy growth, crossing branches and dead wood, or by cutting back to the ground.

Some trees can be hard pruned for foliage effect too, with specimens like the Indian bean tree (*Catalpa bignonioides*) the foxglove tree (*Paulownia tomentosa*) and the tree of heaven (*Ailanthus altissima*) being particularly suitable. This can totally change the dynamics of these plants, turning large flowering trees into plants with huge, lush foliage suitable for a sub-tropical planting or a foliage garden.

Pruning for stem colour

There are many shrubs that are grown for their stem colour effect, including varieties of *Cornus* (dogwood), *Salix* (willow) and *Rubus*. All of these plants require regular pruning if that colour is to be maintained.

Usually this involves hard pruning down to close to the ground – a technique known as "coppicing" – but in the case of some plants, *Salix* in particular, a different effect can be achieved by allowing a single stem or trunk to form and then pruning the top growth back to this trunk. This is called "pollarding".

Coppicing – This is a traditional woodland technique for producing wood that is suitable for fencing, tool handles and so on. By cutting the plant to the ground, long, straight stems form, which are ideal for practical applications. In the garden this technique is most often used to restrict size, and to promote fresh growth in trees and shrubs with colourful stems. Trees that are commonly coppiced include birch (*Betula*), hazel (*Corylus*), hornbeam (*Carpinus*), beech (*Fagus*) and sweet chestnut (*Castanea*).

Pollarding – Often seen along the sides of boulevards and main streets in towns and cities, pollarding involves the hard pruning of the tree crown back to a structure of main branches, to restrict overall size. Over the years these main branches form gnarled stumps. Pollarding also has its roots in woodland management.

Formative pruning

This is all about achieving an attractive shape that will also limit potential weaknesses in growth. These can include crossing branches that rub against each other, and twin leaders – where instead of a single leading stem the plant develops two main shoots which compete with one another. This then leads to a pronounced fork forming between the two stems, which can be prone to rotting and splitting open, causing severe damage.

The key to formative pruning is to achieve a natural, open shape, removing congested branches to help with air circulation and healthy, pest- and disease-free growth. At the same time, it is important to prune out any dead, diseased or damaged wood.

Renovation pruning

Sometimes older shrubs can become misshapen and woody, and you may be tempted to rip the plant out and start again. Before you do this, though, always first consider renovation pruning – cutting the plant back quite hard to a decent framework. When doing this, try to retain some foliage on the lower stems and branches if possible, and after pruning give the plant a good feed and mulch to help boost the chances of re-growth. In situations like this, which require particularly hard pruning, it is very common to worry that you have killed the plant during your ministrations. However, try not to feel guilty – although this will happen occasionally, on the whole the plant will spring back to life within a few weeks or months and will be all the better for the radical surgery you have undertaken.

Correct cutting

Notwithstanding what we said earlier about pruning not being quite as complicated as it is sometimes made out to be, using the correct pruning techniques is essential if the work you carry out is not to compromise the health of your plants.

Removing a branch

To remove a branch from a tree or shrub, first cut the branch back to within 30cm (12in) or so from the trunk. This will remove the weighty part of the branch and will prevent it from tearing. The remaining stub can then be pruned closer to the trunk, but the cut should not be made flush with the trunk. Instead, cut back to the swelling that occurs naturally where the branch extends from the trunk. This will then heal naturally by forming a callus over the cut. It used to be common to seal pruning cuts with a "wound paint" to aid healing, but this has now been proven to exacerbate problems with infection and actually inhibits the healing process. So, leave the cut to heal itself (see oposite).

General pruning

General cuts on trees and shrubs should be made to a bud, which will then grow away without leaving a dead stump. Select a bud that is facing in the direction you want the branch to grow away to, usually outward facing, then make a slanting cut about 50mm (2in) above the bud. Wherever the plant has opposing buds, simply cut straight across.

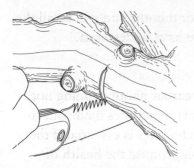 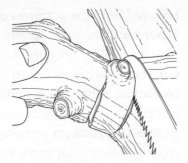

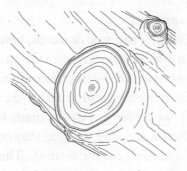

Pruning Hedges

Hedges are planted as windbreaks, boundary markers and security barriers – or they can be installed as a decorative feature in their own right.

The basic technique

Hedges can be pruned with powered hedge trimmers or hand shears, with large leaved evergreen hedges benefiting from a tidy up with secateurs. Regenerative pruning or re-shaping will require the use of bow saws and loppers. To achieve a really level finish to a formal hedge, set up a string line between two posts, the tops of which are the same distance from the ground – check this with a tape measure. Place the string line over the tops of the posts and make sure it is really taut, then use this line as a reference as you cut along the top of the hedge. Mind you don't fall off your stepladder while you're admiring your handiwork!

When to prune

- Deciduous hedges like beech (*Fagus sylvatica*) and hornbeam (*Carpinus betulus*) should be cut in late summer or early autumn.
- Coniferous hedges such as *Taxus baccata* (yew) should be pruned in late summer.
- Evergreen hedges such as box (*Buxus sempervirens*) will need trimming in early summer, ideally on a dry, overcast day when the risk of the exposed cut foliage being scorched is reduced. Other evergreen hedges – laurel, for example – can be pruned in early autumn.
- Hedges that attract lots of wildlife – including species that produce fruit or nuts, which provide a source of winter food – are best trimmed in early spring.

TOP TIPS FOR HEDGE TRIMMING

Birds' nests – Always check for nesting birds before cutting hedges, and never cut in the main nesting season, from early spring to mid-summer. You will generally hear lots of tweeting emanating from the hedge at this time, so simply using your ears will alert you to the presence of birds and will obviate the need for an invasive and potentially alarming physical exploration of the hedge.

Conifer hedges – Do not prune coniferous hedges back too hard, that is into the woody growth, as, with the exception of yew, they will not regenerate. This means that if you get back to the brown, the hedge will stay brown, never becoming green again. Consequently, over-pruning a coniferous hedge can be a pretty serious horticultural error.

Large leaves – Cut large-leaved evergreens with trimmers and then tidy them up with secateurs. It is important to do this and to take care, as large leaves tend to die back and can become unsightly when cut in half by trimmers.

A-shape – Prune hedges into an A-shape – that is, one that is narrower at the top – in order to allow the base of the hedge to remain in light and consequently stay thick and healthy all the way to the ground. In areas that are prone to snowfall in winter, hedges pruned to an A-shape are less likely to collapse under the weight of the snow.

Pruning Climbing Plants

Climbing plants include a wide range of plants with differing pruning requirements, but there are some general tips that can be applied across the group as a whole.

Spur pruning
This method of pruning is a technique that can be applied to a range of plants such as the fruiting vine *Vitis vinifera*, ornamental vines including *Vitis coignetiae* and a range of other climbers including *Actinidia deliciosa* (kiwi fruit).

Although spur pruning is most often applied to vine-like fruiting plants, it is a technique that is equally suitable for many foliage effect vines.

The primary purpose of spur pruning is to create a framework of side shoots from which new flowering and fruiting wood can develop, while providing space within that framework for the fruit to develop fully. After flowering, or more usually during winter or early spring, create the spurs by reducing the side shoots to within three or four buds of the permanent framework.

Reduction pruning

This is a simple technique for restricting the overall size of a climbing plant, which involves trimming the plant back to fit the space available. Carry out pruning during winter or early spring, cutting back side shoots to a bud. In the case of vigorous plants like ivy (*Hedera*), the use of hedge shears or powered hedge trimmers will speed up the job.

Pruning clematis

There are three distinct groups of clematis that require different pruning approaches:

Group one includes the early flowering clematis such as *C. alpina*, *C. armandii* and *C. montana*. Prune plants from this group after flowering, removing dead, damaged and diseased wood and reducing shoots.

Group two are the large-flowered, mid-season flowering plants that include many popular cultivars like *C.* "Nelly Moser" and *C.* "Silver Moon". In early spring before active growth begins, remove any dead, damaged or diseased shoots, and reduce the remaining stems back to a framework of strong buds.

Group three include later flowering clematis, C. "Bill MacKenzie", C. tangutica and the many popular C. *viticella* hybrids; C. "Etoile Violette", C. "Polish Spirit" and many others (check labels when purchasing plants). Prune clematis from this group hard back to within two to three buds from soil level.

Pruning roses

When it comes to pruning, it is roses that seem to worry gardeners most of all. Conventional wisdom has it that anything other than precise cuts as prescribed by immutable rules will spell disaster. Yet roses are far more resilient than is generally believed and will withstand a good deal of hacking about.

The Basics

Rose pruning is often referred to as replacement pruning, because the object of the exercise is to replace old flowering wood with more vigorous new flowering wood. The best time to do this is in winter or early spring when the rose plants are dormant.

Pruning to an outward bud – In most cases, roses should be pruned to an outward facing bud, regardless of the species of rose. A bud is the growing point at which the plant produces leaves or shoots and during winter and early spring, the bud will usually be a modest swelling on the stem. The reason for pruning to an outward facing bud is to create a "goblet" shaped plant with even growth all around the plant.

Pruning after planting – Roses are best planted as bare root plants during the dormant season of winter or early spring. Soon after pruning the plant should be pruned back hard to within five to eight buds from ground level, which will encourage strong new growth to form.

Autumn pruning – Although the main pruning time for roses is winter and early spring, in exposed sites most roses will benefit from reduction in size by around a third in late autumn. This will prevent a phenomenon known as "wind rock", in which top-heavy plants are rocked back and forth by the winter winds, causing the plant to become unstable and risking damage to the stem and root system.

Different types of rose

Bush and cluster-flowered – Of all roses, these are the types that require the hardest pruning. During winter and early spring they should be pruned back to an outward facing bud, to within five to eight buds from the ground.

Shrub roses – After their first full season of growth, shrub roses will benefit from formative pruning. This is rather harder pruning than would take place in subsequent years, and should be aimed at improving the overall shape and structure of the plant. Thereafter, only modest pruning should take place during winter or early spring. Never prune beyond the previous season's growth unless there is a need to remove dead, damaged or diseased material from the plant.

Climbing and rambling roses – Rambling roses produce numerous shoots from ground level, and these should be pruned out, or "replaced", on a regular basis by removing a third of the oldest stems every winter. Climbing roses produce lateral growth – effectively side shoots from the main stem that bear most of the flowering buds – from one or more main stems, and this lateral growth should be regularly pruned back to a framework of outward facing buds.

Pruning Indoor Plants

In general, house plants require little pruning other than a little formative pruning and the removal of dead growth. Formative pruning usually consists of pinching out the growing tip of the plant to encourage bushy, compact growth. This is usually done using thumb and forefinger, pinching and twisting the growing tip – back to a bud – until it detaches, but can be done with sharp scissors or secateurs. This is usually carried out once the plant starts into active growth and begins producing lots of fresh growth. Dead growth can be pruned out at any time, making sure to cut back to a living bud or stem, while dead leaves can normally be pulled off without any difficulty.

Border Maintenance

Alongside pruning, the regular maintenance of garden borders is probably the most important of all gardening tasks. Keeping your ornamental borders in peak condition means ensuring that you are carrying out the right maintenance at the right time of year. In doing so, not only will you ensure that your plants remain healthy and vigorous, you will also understand the yearly round of nature and your entire garden that much better.

Watering

Water has a huge part to play in any garden and is absolutely essential to the growth of all plants. The responsible use of water by gardeners is now more vitally important than ever before, as global warming takes hold, the world population grows exponentially, and water becomes scarcer than in the past. Follow these tips to ensure that you make the best use of water in your garden:

- Do not water at the start of the growing season. Be patient and wait for rain before you resort to watering.
- Consider installing an automated watering system. It will water your plants efficiently and cost effectively.
- One of the most efficient ways to irrigate is to lay a running hose on the border and periodically move it, usually at 10–15 minute intervals.
- Try not to use sprinklers, as they are the least efficient way of irrigating. On a hot day up to 85 per cent of the water will evaporate before it even touches the ground – let alone get taken up by the plant! If you have to use sprinklers, do so only at night.
- Water thoroughly, not little and often. Plants need deep watering when they are under stress, which can mean 15 minutes of water at a good flow rate per plant. A few seconds of water will only damp down the soil

and encourage the plant roots to grow to the surface in search of moisture, where they will be even more vulnerable to drying out.

- Water when the sun goes down. In lower air temperatures evaporation is dramatically reduced, and there is no chance of scorching foliage or flowers.

GARDEN MAINTENANCE THROUGH THE YEAR

Late winter
- Continue pruning shrub, bush, climbing and rambling roses. Tie in ramblers and climbers to a climbing support, or to wires fixed to a wall.
- Prune hedges that have provided fruit and nuts for wildlife over the winter months.
- Spur prune fruiting vines and foliage-effect vines.
- Remove suckering growth from trees and shrubs.
- Plant bare root roses.

Early spring
- Prune foliage-effect shrubs back to a framework. Coppice or hard prune ornamental hazels.
- Prune deciduous winter-flowering Viburnum by removing up to a third of the old flowering wood.
- Prune stem colour shrubs, by hard pruning to within 20cm (8in) of the ground.
- Prune group two and three clematis.
- Prune buddleja species back hard to a framework between 20cm (8in) and 1m (3ft) from the ground.
- Cut back the spent flowering stems and foliage of perennials and grasses.

- Plant autumn-flowering bulbs.
- Cultivate new areas for planting, but only when the ground is neither waterlogged nor frozen.

Mid-spring

Once the risk of frosts has passed, prune the following:

- *Caryopteris clandonensis* cultivars and *Ceratostigma willmottianum* and *plumbaginoides*, back to a framework but not into the previous season's growth.
- *Perovskia* "Blue Spire" to within 20–30cm (8–12in) from the ground.
- Silver foliage effect artemesia, including *Artemesia* "Powis Castle", by trimming lightly.
- Erect support systems for tall growing perennials.
- Divide overgrown clumps of perennials and grasses, and replant or pot on.
- Mulch borders with composted organic matter.

Late spring and early summer

- After flowering, prune group one flowering clematis.
- Deadhead early flowering bulbs, such as daffodils.
- Monitor the new, sappy growth of shrubs and perennials for aphids.
- If frost is likely, protect the flower buds of wisteria with horticultural fleece.
- Tie in the growing stems of climbers such as clematis and climbing roses.
- Plant out hardy plants including perennials and shrubs.
- Plant out annuals and half-hardy perennials, once the risk of late frost has passed.

- Keep on top of weeding.
- Remove the dead foliage of early and mid-season flowering bulbs.

Mid- to late summer
- Prune early-flowering deciduous shrubs.
- Prune evergreen shrubs and begin trimming evergreen hedges and topiary.
- Prune mid-season deciduous shrubs like *Philadelphus*.
- Clip box hedges.
- Deadhead euphorbia.
- Deadhead early flowering perennials such as *Geranium* "Johnson's Blue" and *Nepeta* "Six Hills Giant" by cutting back hard with hedge shears.
- Deadhead repeat-flowering roses to ensure they continue flowering.
- Trim back the current season's growth of English lavender.
- As taller perennials develop, increase the height of staking or plant supports.
- Collect ripened seed from border plants for sowing.

Autumn
- Reduce shrub roses and buddleja by up to one third to reduce wind rock.
- Prune wisteria.
- Trim deciduous hedges that are not being grown for their wildlife benefits.
- Lift and divide perennials.
- Replant existing plants that are incorrectly positioned.

- Mulch thoroughly before the soil becomes damp and cold.
- Plant spring-flowering bulbs (see pages 158–160).
- Plant perennials, grasses, shrubs and trees and in particular bare-root plants from these groups.
- Collect late-ripening seed for sowing.
- Check staking and tree ties on recently planted trees to ensure that they are not "strangling" the tree.

Early to mid-winter
- Begin pruning roses.
- Remove dead, damaged and diseased wood from woody plants.
- Crown lift trees and shrubs.
- Continue planting – especially bare-root trees and shrubs.

Chapter 9

PLANT DIRECTORY: ("TOP TEN OF TEN")

So, you've learnt how to grow it all – now what are you going to grow? Well, here's ten of the very best plants from ten different categories – our definitive "Top Ten of Ten" to get you started. Happy gardening!

Annuals

Agrostemma githago (Corn cockle)
A cornfield annual with long, thin stems and lovely rosy purple flowers. A great plant for the back of the border.
Soil: Any
Aspect: Full sun
Season of interest: Summer
Height and spread: 1m (3ft) plus

Brachyscome hybrids (Swan river daisy)
Australian native annuals with bright daisy flowers in mauve, pink and white. Good for containers.

Soil: Any, fairly fertile
Aspect: Full sun
Season of interest: Summer
Height and spread: 45 x 45cm (18 x 18in)

Convolvulus tricolor
Royal blue or purple petals with fading white or creamy yellow centres. Great plants for a mixed annual border.
Soil: Any
Aspect: Sun
Season of interest: Summer
Height and spread: 50 x 30cm (20 x 12in)

Dianthus barbatus "Summer Sundae"
(Annual Sweet William)
Annual form of the ubiquitous Sweet William, with fragrant multicoloured heads. Excellent border plant. Mixes well with most perennials.
Soil: Any free draining
Aspect: Sun
Season of interest: Summer
Height and spread: 45–60 x 20cm (18–24 x 8in)

Eschscholzia californica (Californian poppy)
American native with beautiful silky-textured, bright orange flowers. Great for combining with grasses in borders.
Soil: Dry, not too fertile
Aspect: Sun
Season of interest: Summer
Height and spread: 30 x 30cm (12 x 12in)

Geranium robertianum (Herb Robert)

Masses of tiny, pink, five-petalled flowers on this invasive annual which is good for gravel and paving cracks.
Soil: Any free draining
Aspect: Sun or part shade
Seasonal interest: Spring, summer, autumn
Height and spread: 20 x 40cm (8 x 16in)

Helianthus annuus (Sunflower)

Biggest of all the hardy annuals, field crop sunflowers are golden yellow, look magnificent but need plenty of room!
Soil: Rich, fertile
Aspect: Sun
Season of interest: Summer
Height and spread: Up to 3 x 1m (10 x 3ft)

Nemesia strumosa (Nemesia)

South African member of the foxglove family, with massed flowers in numerous different colours, including orange, white, red, pink and yellow.
Soil: Any moisture retentive and fertile
Aspect: Sun
Season of interest: Summer
Height and spread: 30 x 15cm (12 x 6in)

Phlox drummondii (Annual phlox)

Pretty, delicate plants with large heads of brightly coloured flowers in lots of different colours. These plants look good with annual grasses.
Soil: Free draining but fertile
Aspect: Sun

Season of interest: Summer
Height and spread: 30 x 30cm (12 x 12in)

Rudbeckia hirta

Lovely yellow and brown daisy flowers with huge centres.
Very flexible plants that go well with lots of perennials in
summer displays.
Soil: Fertile, moisture retentive
Aspect: Sun or part shade
Season of interest: Summer, autumn
Height and spread: 15–60 x 30cm (6–24 x 12in)

Biennials

Angelica gigas (Giant Angelica)

A big, clump-forming plant that can take two or three
years to flower. Large green leaves on purple stems.
Soil: Fertile, not too dry
Aspect: Sun or part shade
Season of interest: Spring, summer, autumn
Height and spread: 2 x 1m (6 x 3ft)

Dianthus chinensis

These hardy biennials grow quickly and make superb
container plants. Lots of brightly coloured flowers with
pink and serrated petals.
Soil: Any free draining
Aspect: Sun
Season of interest: Summer
Height and spread: 30 x 20cm (12 x 8in)

Digitalis (Foxglove)

Beautiful bell-like flowers on long, tall stems. Lots of different colours. Particularly good for adding height to shady borders.
Soil: Any free draining
Aspect: Sun or part shade
Season of interest: Summer
Height and spread: 90 x 50cm (36 x 20in)

Echium pininana (Tower of jewels)

Exotic, strange-looking tall plant with thousands of small, violet-blue or pink flowers. Bees love it.
Soil: Any free draining
Aspect: Sun
Season of interest: Summer
Height and spread: 3 x 1m (10 x 3ft)

Eryngium giganteum "Miss Willmott's Ghost"

Very large biennial with prickly leaves and stems. Silvery-white, thistle-like flowers. These plants make great focal points in borders.
Soil: Any fertile
Aspect: Sun or part shade
Season of interest: Summer, autumn
Height and spread: 150 x 80cm (60 x 32in)

Erysimum (Wallflowers)

Lovely four-petalled blooms in yellow, red, mauve, bronze or cream. These plants are good for dry gravel or Mediterranean-style gardens.
Soil: Free draining

Aspect: Sun
Season of interest: Spring, summer
Height and spread: 75 x 60cm (30 x 24in)

Hesperis matronalis (Sweet rocket)

Lovely, powerfully fragrant blooms in colours ranging
from white through pale mauve to soft purple. Good for
shady borders.
Soil: Any, moist
Aspect: Sun or part shade
Season of interest: Spring, early summer
Height and spread: 90 x 30cm (36 x 12in)

Matthiola incana (Stock)

Highly fragrant single and double blooms in white, violet,
mauve or pink. Stocks have always been popular.
Soil: Any free draining
Aspect: Sun
Season of interest: Summer
Height and spread: 100 x 25cm (39 x 10in)

Myosotis sylvatica (Forget-me-not)

A childhood favourite! Lovely blue, white or pink flowers
that combine perfectly with tulips and many spring
perennials.
Soil: Any well-drained
Aspect: Sun or part shade
Season of interest: Spring, early summer
Height and spread: 30 x 40cm (12 x 16in)

Primula elatior hybrids (Polyanthus)

Close relatives of primroses and cowslips, these fragrant flowers come in lovely shades of yellow, blue, pink, red or white.
Soil: Moist, fertile but well-drained
Aspect: Part shade
Season of interest: Spring
Height and spread: 25 x 25cm (10 x 10in)

Alpines

Aquilegia viridiflora (Columbine)

Characteristic columbine flowers in amazing chocolate-brown, purple and black colours. Delicate and short lived but well worth growing.
Soil: Any, well drained
Aspect: Sun or part shade
Season of interest: Spring
Height and spread: 30 x 20cm (12 x 8in)

Aubrieta x cultorum (Aubretia)

Trailing perennial that loves growing in rock crevices or down walls. Beautiful flowers ranging from violet-blue, through mauve to magenta.
Soil: Dry, limey, well-drained
Aspect: Sun
Season of interest: Spring
Height and spread: 15cm (6in), spreading

Campanula cochlearifolia (Fairy thimbles)

Pretty bellflower species with bright green leaves and lovely light blue flowers. Great for alpine troughs or sinks.

Soil: Any, free draining
Aspect: Sun or part shade
Season of interest: Summer
Height and spread: 15 x 20cm (6 x 8in) and spreading

Euphorbia myrsinites

Superb evergreen with hairless foliage and gold-green flowers. Comes from the Mediterranean, so ideal for a hot, dry bank.
Soil: Very dry
Aspect: Hot sun
Season of interest: Year-round, flowers in spring
Height and spread: 15 x 75cm (6 x 30in), slowly spreading

Gentiana verna (Spring gentian)

Slow-growing perennial with intense blue tubular flowers. Looks good arranged with other early spring alpines.
Soil: Any, but not too dry
Aspect: Sun
Season of interest: Spring
Height and spread: 8 x 15cm (3 x 6in)

Helianthemum "Wisley Primrose" (Rock rose)

A superb rock plant coming in a huge range of colours, including red, pink, cream, bright yellow and orange.
Soil: Dry and hot
Aspect: Full sun
Season of interest: Summer
Height and spread: 25 x 45cm (10 x 18in)

Lewisia cotyledon

Dark green leaves combined with flattened funnel-shaped flowers in hues of pink, orange, purple or yellow make this a very dramatic plant.

Soil: Neutral or acidic, free draining
Aspect: Part shade
Season of interest: Early summer
Height and spread: 30 x 45cm (12 x 18in)

Primula marginata

Lilac-mauve and purple-blue flowers in dramatic clumped heads. Bright green leaves. This plant looks great with any other alpine.

Soil: Any well-drained. Likes lime
Aspect: Full sun in spring, shade in summer
Season of interest: Spring and early summer
Height and spread: 15 x 15cm (6 x 6in)

Ranunculus ficaria (Lesser celandine)

Bright yellow buttercup-like flowers combine with dark green leaves to make this plant a lovely addition to any alpine or woodland garden.

Soil: Not too dry
Aspect: Shade or semi-shade
Season of interest: Early spring
Height and spread: 15 x 30cm (6 x 12in), spreading

Viola riviviana (Dog violet)

Heart-shaped, evergreen leaves combined with small, white, pink or violet blooms that appear in mid-spring make this a perennially popular plant.

Soil: Any

Aspect: Shade, semi-shade
Season of interest: Spring
Height and spread: 15 x 20cm (6 x 8in)

Bulbs

Allium "Purple Giant" (Drumstick allium)
Dramatic-looking member of the onion family with
amazing round purple flower heads on tall, drumstick-like
green stems. A surefire winner.
Soil: Fertile, but free draining
Aspect: Sun or part shade
Season of interest: Early summer
Height and spread: 90 x 20cm (36 x 8in)

Colchicum speciosum (Naked ladies)
Late-summer flowering, crocus-like plant with lilac or mauve
flowers. Looks beautiful naturalized in grass or in a border.
Soil: Any free draining
Aspect: Sun or part shade
Season of interest: Late summer, early autumn
Height and spread: Flowers to 20cm (8in), foliage
45cm (18in)

Crocus speciosus (True autumn crocus)
Violet blue, wine glass-shaped flowers make this a special
autumn plant. The foliage does not appear until late
winter. Showy and elegant.
Soil: Any free draining
Aspect: Sun
Season of interest: Autumn
Height and spread: 12 x 10cm (5 x 4in)

Cyclamen coum

This hardy tuberous perennial flowers in mid-winter or
early spring. Its flowers are beautiful shades of pink, white
and cerise.

Soil: Any, free draining
Aspect: Sun and part shade
Season of interest: Winter, early spring
Height and spread: 10 x 20cm (4 x 8in)

Freesia corymbsa (Freesia)

Everybody loves freesias! This member of the iris family
comes in many different colours, including white, yellow,
mauve, blue or dark mahogany.

Soil: Free draining, sandy
Aspect: Sun
Season of interest: Winter, spring
Height and spread: 45 x 15cm (18 x 6in)

Gladiolus hybrids

A huge group of striking, tall spiky flowers in vivid
purples, pinks, reds, oranges, yellows, greens and whites.
Dramatic and coming back into fashion.

Soil: Free draining
Aspect: Sun
Season of interest: Summer
Height and spread: 100 x 12cm (39 x 5in)

Iris (Dutch hybrids) (Dutch iris)

Irises are hugely popular plants that are largely grown for
the cut flower trade. They have blue, yellow and purple
flowers.

Soil: Fertile, free draining, not too dry

Aspect: Sun
Season of interest: Spring
Height and spread: 45 x 20cm (18 x 8in)

Lilium hybrids

Lilies bear dramatic, often highly scented flowers and are excellent container plants. They combine well with many plants.
Soil: Fertile but free draining
Aspect: Sun or part shade
Season of interest: Summer, autumn
Height and spread: 50 x 75cm (20 x 30in)

Narcissus (Daffodil)

Among the most popular of hardy bulbs, daffodils come in literally hundreds of different varieties. No spring garden is really complete without them.
Soil: Any, not too dry
Aspect: Sun or part shade
Season of interest: Spring
Height and spread: 30 x 12cm (12 x 5in)

Tulipa (Tulip)

Everyone's spring favourite! Unlimited colours, shapes and varieties. Have some fun growing tulips in your garden.
Soil: Fertile, free draining
Aspect: Sun or part shade
Season of interest: Spring
Height and spread: 25 x 15cm (10 x 6in)

Perennials

Achillea millefolium (Yarrow)

A common wild herb, with deeply divided foliage and huge flower heads. Comes in a range of colours from pale yellow through apricot orange.
Soil: Any free draining
Aspect: Sun
Season of interest: Summer, autumn
Height and spread: 75 x 60cm (30 x 24in)

Agapanthus (African lily)

Glossy, strap-like leaves and amazing blue, funnel-shaped flowers. This African native is a superb container plant and also very good in a mixed border.
Soil: Fertile, free draining
Aspect: Sun, partial shade
Season of interest: Summer
Height and spread: 90 x 45cm (36 x 18in)

Anemone x hybrida (Japanese anemones)

These anemones, also known as summer anemones, have large pink, white or rose-coloured flowers with bold yellow centres.
Soil: Any free draining
Aspect: Sun, part shade, shade
Season of interest: Late summer, autumn
Height and spread: Up to 2m (6ft), spreading

Clematis

Really the king of climbing plants, clematis comes in so many different species and varieties that you can have one

growing all year round.
Soil: Any
Aspect: Sun
Season of interest: Year-round
Height and spread: Variable

Helleborus orientalis hybrids
These hardy perennials come in a wide range of colours, shapes and sizes. The flowers may be white, shades of pink and purple, yellow or bright green.
Soil: Fertile, not too dry, yet well-drained
Aspect: Shade, part shade
Season of interest: Winter, spring, early summer
Height and spread: 40 x 45cm (16 x 18in)

Hosta
These are great plants for any garden, with highly decorative foliage and wonderful shapes. You should have at least one hosta in your garden.
Soil: Fertile
Aspect: Shade, part shade
Season of interest: Spring, summer, autumn
Height and spread: Variable

Osteospermum Symphony Series
Modern hybrids of South African daisies, these plants are particularly good for container use. Lovely flowers in shades of orange, apricot and cream.
Soil: Any fertile, free draining
Aspect: Sun
Season of interest: Summer
Height and spread: 45 x 45cm (18 x 18in)

Potentilla recta (Upright cinquefoil)

A tall, handsome plant with five-petalled, rose-like flowers in bright golden yellow. Blends well with other plants in borders.

Soil: Any
Aspect: Sun
Season of interest: Summer
Height and spread: 60 x 60cm (24 x 24in)

Verbena "Homestead Purple"

A superb, highly vigorous perennial with huge umbels of bright purple flowers. A real eye-catcher. Particularly good for containers.

Soil: Any, reasonably fertile
Aspect: Sun
Season of interest: Summer, autumn
Height and spread: 45cm (18in), spreading

Viola hybrid cultivars (Pansies)

Everybody loves pansies. They provide an almost constant succession of flowers in the distinctive viola shape. There are countless colours available.

Soil: Any, reasonably fertile, free draining
Aspect: Sun, part shade. Not too hot
Season of interest: Year-round
Height and spread: 20 x 25cm (8 x 10in)

Shrubs

Abutilon vitifolium
This fast-growing, short-lived shrub has an open habit and large vine-like leaves. Produces masses of pinkish-mauve flowers.
Soil: Any, free draining
Aspect: Full sun
Season of interest: Summer
Height and spread: 4 x 2.5m (13 x 8ft)

Berberis dictophylla
A thorny, strong-growing shrub, this has an interesting pale blueish-grey colour. Bright red berries and foliage in the autumn.
Soil: Any free draining, not too dry
Aspect: Sun or part shade
Season of interest: Year-round
Height and spread: 2 x 1.5m (6 x 5ft)

Buddleja davidii (Butterfly bush)
A large Chinese shrub with fragrant, densely crowded mauve flowers, each with a pinprick orange centre. Irresistible to butterflies.
Soil: Any free draining
Aspect: Sun
Season of interest: Summer
Height and spread: Variable to 6 x 3m (20 x 10ft)

Ceanothus x delileanus "Gloire de Versailles" (California lilac)
A slow-growing shrub with dark green leaves and

amazing, smoky-blue flowers that are produced in huge quantities.
Soil: fertile, well-drained
Aspect: Sun
Season of interest: Summer, autumn
Height and spread: 1.5 x 1.5m (5 x 5ft)

Cytisus scoparius (Common broom)
An erect, slightly untidy shrub with dark evergreen stems and masses of buttercup-yellow pea flowers. Looks good in the back of a border.
Soil: Free draining, acidic, not too fertile
Aspect: Sun
Season of interest: Early summer
Height and spread: 2 x 1.5m (6 x 5ft)

Hamamelis x intermedia (Witch hazel)
Unusual shrub with spreading branches and weird, spidery, fragrant flowers. Amazing autumn colour.
Soil: Humus rich, well-drained, reasonably fertile
Aspect: Partial shade
Season of interest: Winter, autumn
Height and spread: 4 x 3m (13 x 10ft)

Hydrangea macrophylla (Garden hydrangea)
Very showy shrub with huge mop-heads of flowers – blue in acid soils, pink in alkaline soils. A favourite!
Soil: Any fertile, not to dry
Aspect: Sun, but not too hot, or semi-shade
Season of interest: Summer, autumn
Height and spread 2.5 x 2m (8 x 6ft)

Lonicera x purpusii (Winter honeysuckle)

A vigorous shrub with woody stems and oval, pointed leaves. Produces intensely fragrant cream flowers during mild spells in winter.

Soil: Any free draining, not too dry
Aspect: Sun, part shade or shade
Season of interest: Winter
Height and spread: 3 x 2.5m (10 x 8ft)

Mahonia lomariifolia

A very prickly, erect shrub that produces bright yellow, fragrant flowers. Good for deterring intruders!

Soil: Any reasonably fertile, free draining but not too dry
Aspect: Sun or part shade
Season of interest: Year-round
Height and spread: 3 x 2m (10 x 6ft)

Photinia x fraseri

Beautiful shrub with waxy, oval leaves and amazing red colour. Produces cream-coloured flowers, but it is the foliage that everyone raves about.

Soil: Any reasonably fertile
Aspect: Sun or part shade
Season of interest: Year-round
Height and spread: 4.5 x 4m (15 x 13ft)

Trees

Acer griseum (Paperback maple)

A rounded, spreading tree with the most amazing tan-coloured, peeling, papery bark. Fantastic orange leaf colour in the autumn.

Soil: Any free draining, not too dry
Aspect: Sun or part shade, must be sheltered
Season of interest: Year-round, autumn
Height and spread: 12 x 10m (40 x 33ft)

Alnus glutinosa (Common alder)

A fast-growing, medium-sized tree that produces golden
catkins. Good planted with willows to form a shelter belt.
Soil: Any not too dry
Aspect: Some part shade
Season of interest: Year-round
Height and spread: 18 x 10m (60 x 33ft)

Betula pendula (European silver birch)

A fast-growing, beautiful tree with lovely silver bark
and emerald green leaves that turn yellow before falling.
Produces short hanging catkins.
Soil: Any
Aspect: Sun, part shade
Season of interest: Year-round
Height and spread: 24 x 8m (80 x 25ft)

Cryptomeria japonica (Japanese cedar)

A small, distinctive conifer with lovely curling foliage
that is soft to the touch. Looks great with succulents and
architectural plants.
Soil: Any
Aspect: Sun or part shade
Season of interest: Year-round
Height and spread: Up to 30m (100ft), but garden forms
smaller

Juniperus communis (Common juniper)

A handsome little conifer with a narrow, upright outline.
Produces distinctive berries, in a blue and silvery colour.
Soil: Any free draining
Aspect: Sun or part shade
Season of interest: Year-round
Height and spread: Up to 6 x 1m (20 x 3ft)

Magnolia x soulangeana

A splendid garden magnolia with large, tulip-shaped
white and pink flowers. Goes well with any spring flowers
at its feet.
Soil: Any free draining, not too dry
Aspect: Sun or part shade
Season of interest: Spring
Height and spread: 6 x 6m (20 x 20ft)

Pyrus salicifolia (Willow leaved pear)

A graceful little tree with dense growth and downy, pale
grey-green leaves. Produces white blossoms during the
spring and summer.
Soil: Any free draining
Aspect: Sun, part shade
Season of interest: Spring, summer, autumn
Height and spread: 8 x 4m (25 x 12ft)

Rhus typhina (Stag's horn sumach)

This small tree produces copious suckers on its stiff,
wide branching stems, but its velvety texture and superb
autumn foliage make it a worthwhile contender.
Soil: Any

Aspect: Sun or part shade
Season of interest: Year-round
Height and spread: 5 x 5m (16 x 16ft)

Salix exigua (Coyote willow)

A truly beautiful small tree with silvery grey leaves that waft on long tapering branches. Produces greenish-yellow catkins in mid-spring.
Soil: Any well-drained
Aspect: Sun, part shade
Season of interest: Summer, autumn
Height and spread: 4 x 5m (13 x 16ft)

Trachycarpus fortunei (Chusan palm)

A very hardy garden palm, producing huge fan-shaped, dark green, glossy fronds. Also sprouts greenish-yellow flowers and purplish-black fruits.
Soil: Any free draining
Aspect: Sun or part shade
Season of interest: Year-round
Height and spread: 10 x 2.5m (33 x 8ft)

Ferns

Asplenium nidus (Bird's nest fern)

A large, evergreen fern with broad, oar-shaped leaves in a rich, iridescent green. A lovely plant, but it doesn't like frost!
Soil: Humus rich
Aspect: Shade or part shade
Season of interest: Year-round
Height and spread: 1.5 x 1m (5 x 3ft)

Asplenium scolopendrium (Hart's tongue fern)

Not particularly fern-like, but very attractive nonetheless!
Glossy, tongue-shaped leaves spring from a broad base.
Looks good with spring flowers.
Soil: Any well-drained
Aspect: Shade or part shade
Season of interest: Year-round
Height and spread: 30 x 30cm (12 x 12in)

Asplenium trichomanes (Maidenhair spleenwort)

A tiny fern that does well planted in nooks and crannies,
for example in old walls.
Soil: Very free draining
Aspect: Shade or part shade
Season of interest: Year-round
Height and spread: 15cm (6in), spreading

Blechnum discolor (Crown fern)

Unusual fern with symmetrical rosettes of fronds that are
pale green when new, darkening to a rich glossy green as
they mature.
Soil: Humus rich, lime free
Aspect: Shade
Season of interest: Year-round
Height and spread: 40 x 40cm (16 x 16in)

Blechnum spicant (Hard fern)

A clump-forming, evergreen fern that loves the shade.
Looks great with early shrubs such as camellia or
rhododendrons.
Soil: Lime-free soil, well drained

Aspect: Shade or part shade
Season of interest: Year-round
Height and spread: 45 x 30cm (18 x 12in)

Dicksonia antarctica (Tree fern)
The giant fern, heralding from Australasia. Difficult to
grow, as it prefers cool, moist conditions, but well worth
the effort if you can be bothered.
Soil: Any humus rich
Aspect: Shade
Season of interest: Year-round
Height and spread: 3 x 2m (10 x 6ft)

Dryopteris wallichiana (Wallich's wood fern)
A large, beautiful deciduous fern which looks like a
small tree fern. Striking yellow green foliage. Great for a
woodland or shaded garden.
Soil: Moist
Aspect: Shade or part shade
Season of interest: Spring, summer
Height and spread 1.5 x 1m (5 x 3ft)

Matteuccia struthiopteris (Ostrich plume fern)
A big, striking fern which produces huge green
shuttlecocks of foliage in the spring. Goes well with bog
plants.
Soil: Moist, leafy soil
Aspect: Part shade, shade or sun
Season of interest: Spring, summer
Height and spread: 1 x 0.6m (3 x 2ft)

Polystichum munitum (Sword fern)

An evergreen fern with broad fronds, toothy leaves and blunt ends. This is a good-looking plant that is a useful addition to any shady garden.

Soil: Any, humus rich
Aspect: Shade, part shade
Season of interest: Year-round
Height and spread: 1 x 1.5m (3 x 5ft)

Polystichum polyblepharum (Japanese tassel fern)

This evergreen fern looks elegant all year round. It has an intricate outline that looks good combined with spring bulbs in containers.

Soil: Humus rich, not to dry
Aspect: Shade or part shade
Season of interest: Year-round
Height and spread: 75 x 90cm (30 x 36in)

Climbers

Billardiera longiflora (Climbing blueberry)

This native of Tasmania and Australia has slender, twining stems and simple leaves. It produces superb tubular, greenish flowers in summer followed by oblong berries.

Soil: Well drained
Aspect: Sun
Season of interest: Summer, autumn
Height and spread: 2 x 1m (6 x 3ft)

Campsis radicans

A very vigorous, woody climber, with clusters of pinky-red flowers that look like lobster claws. Great teamed with wisteria.

Soil: Any free draining
Aspect: Sun
Season of interest: Summer, autumn
Height and spread: 5 x 5m (15 x 15ft)

Cobaea scandens (Cathedral bell)

This vigorous perennial climber produces huge, bell-shaped flowers that are green when young, turning purple or white as they age.
Soil: Any fertile, free draining
Aspect: Sun, part shade
Season of interest: Summer, autumn
Height and spread: Up to 10m (33ft), spreading

Euonymus fortunei

A beautiful green climber with small, oval leaves. Produces tiny, greenish-yellow flowers in the summer.
Soil: Any
Aspect: Sun or part shade
Season of interest: Year-round
Height and spread: 0.3 x 3m (1 x 10ft) and spreading

Hedera helix (English ivy)

There are lots of different types of English ivy, which while it is invasive is incredibly decorative. Lovely colours and interesting berries.
Soil: Any
Aspect: Any
Season of interest: Year-round
Height and spread: Almost unlimited

Jasminum nudiflorum (Winter jasmine)

This classic garden plant can be used either as a climber or for ground cover. Produces bright yellow flowers opening in pairs along young stems.

Soil: Any
Aspect: Sun, part shade or shade
Season of interest: Winter
Height and spread: 3 x 3m (10 x 10ft)

Parthenocissus quinquefolia (Virginia creeper)

The classic autumn climber, producing magnificent autumnal hues of fiery red and green. Invasive, but so good-looking that it's worth having in any garden!

Soil: Not too dry
Aspect: Sun or part shade
Season of interest: Summer, autumn
Height and spread: Spreading. Almost unlimited

Passiflora caerulea (Blue passion flower)

This tendril climber has interesting leaves and purplish stems, but the main draw is the incredibly distinctive blossoms that are produced in summer.

Soil: Any
Aspect: Sun or part shade
Season of interest: Summer, autumn
Height and spread: To 6m (20ft)

Rosa "Alister Stella Gray"

A lovely, fragrant climbing rose, which produces beautiful pale lemon blooms with dark yellow centres. One of the most attractive climbing roses.

Soil: Heavy, not too dry

Aspect: Sun
Season of interest: Summer
Height and spread: To 5m (15ft), spreading

Wisteria floribunda (Japanese wisteria)
In spring this woody, deciduous climber produces amazing racemes of gently scented, violet blue pea flowers. You need a big wall for this plant!
Soil: Any free draining
Aspect: Sun
Season of interest: Spring
Height and spread: More than 10m (33ft), spreading

Indoor Plants

Aspidistra elatior (Cast-iron plant)
If you are after a tough houseplant, look no further than the aspidistra. Dark green shiny leaves, some speckled with white. A great indoor plant.
Soil: Moist
Aspect: Partial shade
Season of interest: Year-round
Height and spread: 45 x 45cm (18 x 18in)

Begonia x *hiemalis* (Winter-flowering begonia)
Despite its name, this plant actually flowers all year round. It comes in masses of colours, from white to pink, and yellow-orange to red.
Soil: Moist
Aspect: Sun, but not too hot
Season of interest: Year-round
Height and spread: 45 x 45cm (18 x 18in)

Caladium bicolor (**Elephant's ear**)
This dramatic houseplant has heart-shaped leaves that come in bright crimson, white and green. This plant needs careful attention but is worth the effort.
Soil: Very moist. Needs feeding
Aspect: Indirect sunlight
Height and spread: 45 x 60cm (18 x 24in)

Callistemon citrinus (**Bottle brush**)
This very attractive shrub makes a good conservatory plant. It produces brilliant, crimson-red spikes on the end of shoots in the spring and summer.
Soil: Moist. Needs feeding
Aspect: Sun
Season of interest: Spring, summer
Height and spread: 90 x 30cm (36 x 12in)

Campanula isophylla (**Star of Bethlehem**)
A very pretty trailing plant that looks good tumbling from a pot or hanging basket. Produces star-shaped flowers in violet-blue throughout summer and autumn.
Soil: Very moist
Aspect: Indirect sunlight
Season of interest: Summer, autumn
Height and spread: 30 x 30cm (12 x 12in)

Dahlia hybrida "Dahlietta" (**Pot dahlia**)
These are easy to grow, small forms of dahlia, with superb double flowers in white and shades of pink, red, orange and yellow.
Soil: Moist

Aspect: Indirect sunlight
Season of interest: Year-round
Height and spread: 30 x 30cm (12 x 12in)

Echeveria agavoides (Echeveria)
This fleshy, succulent plant looks pretty in a pot
surrounded by gravel. Be careful not to over-water it,
as it will rot.
Soil: Moist
Aspect: Sun
Season of interest: Year-round
Height and spread: 15 x 15cm (6 x 6in)

Euphorbia pulcherrima (Poinsettia)
The poinsettia has become the ultimate Christmas plant,
thanks to its cheerful, brightly coloured scarlet flower
heads. A lovely houseplant.
Soil: Moist
Aspect: Indirect sunlight
Season of interest: Winter
Height and spread: 30 x 30cm (12 x 12in)

Fuchsia spp. (Ladies' eardrops)
You can grow fuchsias pretty much anywhere, but the
small varieties make particularly attractive houseplants.
Prolific flowers in bright reds and purples.
Soil: Moist
Aspect: Indirect sunlight
Season of interest: Year-round
Height and spread: Variable

Portuluca grandiflora (Purslane)

A semi-succulent plant grown for its showy, cup-shaped blooms in white, yellow, apricot, pink, red and purple. Can be mound forming or trailing.
Soil: Moist
Aspect: Sun
Season of interest: Summer
Height and spread: 30 x 35cm (12 x 14in)

APPENDICES

Pests, Diseases and Problems

You are not the only one who can suffer from ill-health – so can your garden! Unlike yourself, it is not necessarily age that will cause problems in your garden, but inevitably, any garden will suffer occasional difficulties that affect the quality and growth of plants and crops. Part of this is due to the very nature of garden plants, many of which are naturalized and non-native, therefore bringing with them their own range of problems that are sometimes exacerbated in a garden setting.

Pests can range from specific insect pests that affect only one group of plants, such as lily beetle, to non-specific pests that might trouble a range of plants – slugs and snails, for example. Most plant diseases are either fungal or viral. Fungal diseases are often associated with weather conditions, either damp and warm or on occasion excessively hot, and can be passed from plant to plant by pollinating insects. Viral conditions are also often spread from plant to plant by insects. Excessive heat, wind and over saturation are all cultural problems that can also damage and kill plants. Poor nutrient levels and inadequate soil cultivation will also normally have an adverse effect on plant growth and health. Weeds – which are basically unwanted plants – exacerbate cultural problems, as they compete with garden plants for nutrients, water, light and space.

Pests

Many of the problems that affect plants can be offset in the earliest stages of establishing a garden, simply by the way that plants are grouped together, and how they are planted and maintained. For example, a garden that has one predominant plant – say, roses – will always be prone to specific diseases, whereas a garden with a mixture of plants tends to be more balanced and less likely to suffer problems. In this respect plants are rather like human beings: the less in-bred they are, the better their health! Keep these simple rules of thumb in mind and your garden will be less likely to suffer from problems:

- Choose plants which are suitable for your garden's aspect, soil and weather conditions.
- Cultivate your soil thoroughly and install your plants properly.
- Try to avoid plantings dominated by one type of plant, as mixed plantings tend to be far healthier.
- Tend your plants carefully in times of extreme weather, as a stressed plant is more likely to suffer from pests or diseases than a healthy one.
- Try to anticipate problems before they occur, through regular and careful inspection of your garden. This will save time and effort later on. In any garden, the earlier a problem can be tackled, the greater the chances of success.

GLOSSARY

Acid – a pH value of below 7.0.

Aeration – improving soil air circulation by mechanically loosening the soil.

Aerial root – a root that forms above the ground on a stem.

Alkaline – a pH value above 7.0.

Alpine – a high-altitude plant, suitable for rock gardens.

Annual – a plant completing its life cycle within one growing season.

Aquatic plant – a plant that grows in or floats on water.

Basal – at the base of a structure or organ, for example a leaf or stem.

Berry – the fruit surrounding a seed or seeds.

Biennial – a plant that completes its life cycle in two years by growing in the first year and flowering in the second.

Biological control – a naturally occurring or introduced control for pests, normally in the form of nematodes or insect predators.

Bloom – flower or blossom, or a white, powdery coating found on some plants.

Bog garden – a waterlogged area suitable for plants that thrive in permanently moist soil.

Bottom heat – a method employed in propagation, heating provided at the root zone to encourage rooting.

Bract – a modified leaf at the base of a flower designed to look like a large flower or petal.

Bud – the organ enclosing the immature stage of a leaf, flower, shoot.

Bulb – a modified bud growing below ground.

Bulblet – small bulb formed at the side of the parent.

Catkin – a form of inflorescence consisting of bracts and tiny flowers, usually arranged in a pendant form.

Chalky – a soil with a high level of calcium carbonate (chalk) or magnesium carbonate.

Chlorophyll – the green pigment that absorbs energy from sunlight.

Chlorosis – the loss of chlorophyll leading to leaf discolouration – yellowing – caused by mineral deficiency, disease or low light levels.

Clay – fertile, heavy soil that is moisture retentive and prone to compaction and capping.

Climber – a plant that clings or climbs by using modified stems, leaves, roots or leaf stalks.

Coppice – to prune shrubs or trees to ground level to promote strong regeneration.

Cordon – a plant trained and restricted to one stem.

Corm – a below-ground storage organ.

Cross – interbreeding, hybridization between two or more plants.

Crown – the growing point of a plant from which new stems grow, or, the upper foliage and framework of a tree or large shrub.

Cultivar – a cultivated variety of a species.

Cutting – a section of stem, leaf or root used for propagation.

Damp down – wetting the floor of a greenhouse or conservatory to boost humidity and reduce temperatures.

Damping off – a fungal disease causing the rotting and collapse of seedlings.

Deadhead – removing old and spent flowers/flower heads to promote further flowering or prevent seed setting.

Deciduous – plants that shed seeds annually.

Divide – propagation of plants (usually perennials) by dividing the parent crown into several sections.

Dwarf – a small or slow-growing form of plant.

Epiphyte – a plant that grows on another without acting as a parasite by taking food or water.

Ericaceous – acid loving plant/compost, plant from the family Ericaceae.

Espalier – a method of training fruit into a tree with pairs of horizontal branches from a main trunk.

Evergreen – a plant that retains its leaves over more than one season, or which retains most of its leaves over that period.

Family – primary category in plant classification, coming between order and genus.

Feathered (as in feathered maiden) – a tree with a main trunk and lateral branches furnished to the ground.

Fern – a non-flowering vascular plant, frequently with feathery fronds.

Fertilization – the sexual fusion of male and female plant elements that initiates the development of seed.

Fertilizer – organic or inorganic compounds added to the growing media to improve/alter nutrient levels.

Flower – the reproductive structure of flowering plants.

Frond – the leaf of a fern.

Fungus – non-photosynthetic, non-vascular organism including mushrooms, moulds.

Garden origin – applies to plants that have been artificially bred or selected.

Genus – primary category in plant classification, ranked between family and species.

Germination – the change that occurs when a seed develops into a young plant.

Glaucous – covered with a blue/green or blue/grey bloom.

Growing season – the part of the year in which active plant growth occurs.

Grow on – the stage after propagation when plants have been potted on and are grown for a further period before planting.

Habit – the appearance or growing tendency of a plant that gives it its characteristic form.

Harden off – to gradually acclimatize plants that have been raised in a greenhouse to the external environment.

Hardiness – the measure of reliance to frosts displayed by plants.

Hardwood – mature wood used for cutting material.

Herb – a plant with practical applications such as culinary or medicinal, or in botany any herbaceous plant.

Herbaceous – a plant that dies back to ground level at the end of the growing season and regenerates from the crown the following season.

Herbicide – chemicals used in weed control.

Humidity – the measure of air moisture content.

Humus – decomposed organic matter found in or introduced into soil/growing media.

Hybrid – a natural or artificially produced plant with two genetically distinct parents.

Infertile – soil low in nutrients or plants that do not flower due to cultural problems, disease or pests.

Inflorescence – arrangement of flowers on a single stem or axis.

Internode – a section of stem between two nodes.

Insecticide – chemical used to control insect pests.

Invasive – an aggressive plant that invades or overwhelms other plants.

Lateral – side shoot from the stem of the main plant.

Layering – a method of propagation where an attached stem is encouraged to root by laying and fixing on the soil.

Leader – the main growing stem of a plant.

Leaf – plant organ that is the primary organ in photosynthesis.

Liquid feed – a fertilizer diluted in water for application.

Loam – fertile, well-drained but moisture-retentive soil.

Marginal – a plant requiring permanently moist conditions, as found at the edge of a water course.

Mist – a method of increasing humidity by spraying fine droplets of water into the atmosphere or onto a plant.

Mulch – a layer of material spread on the soil surface to suppress weeds and/or improve fertility.

Native – an endemic plant that occurs naturally in an area/country.

Naturalized – introduced plants that grow as if native.

Nectar – sugary liquid secreted by some plants to attract pollinators.

Neutral – a pH of 7.0, i.e. neither acid nor alkaline.

Node – the point on a stem at which leaves, leaf buds and shoots arise.

Nut – dry fruit surrounding a single seed.

Nutrients – the minerals needed for healthy plant growth.

Offset – a small plant that forms naturally as part of a plant's vegetative growth.

Oxygenator – a fully submerged aquatic plant that releases oxygen into the water.

Pan – a shallow dish used for growing alpines.

Panicle – term applied to plants with freely branched inflorescences.

Parasite – a plant that derives nutrients from another plant.

Peat – humus-rich, moisture-retentive decayed organic matter with a pH below 6.5.

Perennial – a plant that lives for more than two growing seasons.

Pesticide – chemicals used to control insect pests.

Petal – a modified leaf that makes up part of the flower.

pH – measure of acidity or alkalinity.

Photosynthesis – the complex series of chemical reactions in which energy from sunlight is absorbed by chlorophyll and carbon dioxide and water converted into sugars and oxygen.

Plantlet – a young, small plant that develops alongside an older one.

Pollard – to cut branches back hard to a framework or to the main trunk of a tree to restrict growth.

Pollen – grains containing the male element needed for fertilization.

Prick out – the transfer of seedlings or small cuttings into larger pots or containers.

Propagate – to increase plants by seed, cuttings, etc.

Prostrate – a plant with stems that trail or lie flat against the ground.

Respiration – absorption of oxygen and breakdown of carbohydrates, releasing carbon dioxide and water and providing energy for the plant.

Rhizome – horizontal, branching or fleshy stem growing underground or at ground level.

Rock garden – area for growing alpine plants.

Root – part of the plant that anchors it and absorbs water and nutrients from the soil or to successfully strike cuttings.

Rootball – a mass of roots and the compost or soil attached to them.

Rootstock – the underground part of a plant or the plant onto which another is grafted, as in fruit trees, roses, etc.

Rosette – the dense whorl of leaves arising from a central point or crown of a plant.

Sap – the watery fluid that runs through the conductive tissue of plants.

Scarify – removal of moss, weeds and thatch from a lawn by mechanical abrasion.

Seed head – the dried fruits of, for example, perennials.

Seedling – a young plant raised from seed.

Shoot – side growth, branch, twig or stem.

Shrub – a deciduous or evergreen woody plant with multiple stems.

Silt – moderately fertile moisture retentive soil prone to capping and compaction.

Softwood – the soft, young unripened wood of trees and shrubs.

Specimen plant – a plant grown in a prominent position, alone or with a low planting, which can be viewed from multiple angles.

Species – basic category of plant classification, ranked below genus.

Spur – short branches or branchlets along the main stem on which flowers and fruit are produced.

Standard – a tree or shrub that has been trained with a clear stem and head of foliage.

Stem – the main part of a plant, from which side stems form.

Sterile – a flower that cannot produce seeds or soil that is lacking in nutrients or has been treated to kill weed seeds.

Succulent – a plant with fleshy leaves and stems, often native to dry areas.

Tap root – a primary root, often swollen, from which the secondary root system develops.

Terminal – the end point of a stem, shoot.

Terrestrial – a plant that grows in soil.

Topiary – the clipping and training of plants into architectural or representational forms.

Train – the pruning and shaping of a tree or shrub.

Transpiration – the evaporation of water from the leaves of a plant.

Tree – a woody perennial with a crown of branches developing from a single trunk.

Variegation – the irregular pigmentation in a leaf caused by mutation or disease.

Variety – a naturally occurring variation of a species.

Vascular – containing conductive tissue that enable the passage of sap in a plant.

Waterlogged – soil that is saturated with water.

Weed – vigorous, invasive plant or any plant growing where it is not wanted.

INDEX

Index